THE ULTIMATE SERIAL KILLER TRIVIA BOOK

A Collection Of Fascinating Facts And
Disturbing Details About Infamous
Serial Killers And Their Horrific Crimes

Jack Rosewood

ISBN: 978-1-64845-089-1

FREE BONUS!

CONTENTS

INTRODUCTION

The serial killer is an enigmatic creature, unknowable to the rational thinker. For decades, serial killers have fascinated and disturbed us with their monstrous actions, stalking the shadows, taking lives, and feeling no remorse for their crimes. While they might look like human beings on the surface, there's something in the serial killer's mind that makes them uniquely 'Other'.

The serial killer has no awareness of the consequences. Instead, his (or her) primary aim is to indulge their sadistic desires, quench their bloodlust, and bask in the high of playing God. Each serial killer has unique reasons for doing what they do, many of which are unfathomable to the non-psychopathic mind. These predators, despite exhibiting calm and purposeful behavior on the surface, are masters of cunning and manipulation. Serial killers possess what psychologists term as "predatory aggressive personalities," which makes them believe that everyone else is inferior, therefore justifying their acts of brutality upon their unsuspecting victims.

But while we might understand the basics of serial killer psychopathology, or perhaps even consider ourselves experts in the field, there's also a lot that most people *don't* know. There's a treasure trove of true crime information out there, much of which

1

people with a significant "cooling-off period" of more than 30 days between each murder. However, the definition has recently changed from three victims to two.

There are also arguments that serial killing is more of a mindset than a series of physical acts. For example, if an offender was caught after committing a single murder, but had intentions of carrying out more, should they also be classified as a serial killer despite their victim count not reaching the required level? Regardless, the above definition is considered to be official as of September 2022.

Who coined the term "serial killer"?

The common belief is that FBI Special Agent Robert Ressler invented the term "serial killer" during a lecture on criminal profiling in the late 1970s. The agent, famous for his work in the field of criminal psychology and considered to be the father of modern behavioral profiling, allegedly used the term when referring to New York serial killer David Berkowitz.

However, there are a number of documented uses of the same (or similar) terms dating back decades before Ressler mentioned it in the 1970s. In Dorothy B. Hughes's mystery book *A Lonely Place* (1947), Hughes refers to the antagonist as a "series killer."

Perhaps the earliest usage of the term comes in 1930 from Ernst August Ferdinand Gennat, a famous German detective who revolutionized police work by introducing what modern standards might call Behavioral profiling. In 1930, Gennat wrote extensively about famous German serial killer Peter Kürten in his publication, *Die Düsseldorfer Sexualverbrechen*. Here, Gennat used the term "Serienmörder," which translates in English to "serial murderer," but more colloquially as "serial killer."

Despite Gennat's revolutionary approach, his work in the field of behavioral profiling didn't garner as much acclaim as Ressler's did 40 years later. It may have been that Ressler was inspired by Gennat given the similarities in their work.

What are the four "types" of a serial killer?

Generally, serial killers are broken down into four distinct types: Visionary, Mission-oriented, Hedonistic, and Power/Control. These "types" are compartmentalized based on a killer's motivations rather than any physical aspect of their crimes, as follows:

- ✦ Visionary - Believes that a separate entity is commanding them to kill
- ✦ Mission-oriented - Murders as a way to rid society of a particular group of people
- ✦ Hedonistic - Kills for their own personal satisfaction, often sexually motivated
- ✦ Power/Control - Craves domination over their victims, so kills in order to "own" them.

What are some examples of a Visionary serial killer?

One of the most famous Visionary serial killers of all time is Richard Chase, also known as the Vampire of Sacramento. Chase, a deluded psychotic, believed that his blood was slowly turning to powder and that the only way to replenish it was to consume the blood of others. Between 1977 and 1978, Chase murdered 13 people throughout Sacramento, California.

Chase was a strange child and an even stranger adult. His obsession with blood began at a young age, devouring animals, butchering their carcasses, and consuming their raw entrails. As an adult, Chase was discovered in a variety of bizarre situations, including being discovered naked in a field covered in cow's blood. His delusions only increased as he grew older. He began to believe that the bones in his skull were gradually falling apart. He injected himself with rabbit's blood to keep his supply topped up. He was eventually put into a psychiatric hospital in his late twenties.

In 1977, Chase entered the realm of murder, stabbing and shooting hapless victims around Sacramento. He wasn't concerned with their age, race, or gender, only their deaths. In the case of several victims, he drank their blood and ate their remains.

When police uncovered Chase as a suspect, they found jars of human blood in his apartment, as well as blood-stained clothing. Chase was arrested, charged with six counts of murder, and eventually sentenced to death. He died in his prison cell of an overdose on Boxing Day 1980.

What are some examples of a Mission-oriented serial killer?

Peter Sutcliffe, aka the Yorkshire Ripper, is a perfect example of a mission-oriented serial killer. Sutcliffe was once belittled by a sex worker, and so between 1975 and 1980, he attacked and killed a total of 13 sex workers and attempted to murder seven others between 1975 and 1980 throughout the North of England.

Like many other mission-oriented killers, Sutcliffe targeted a particular race, age, and gender (white, young, female) and kept his killings confined to a small geographic region. He also kept his modus operandi consistent throughout his entire killing spree, blitz-attacking women with his weapon of choice: a hammer. Upon his capture, Sutcliffe famously said that he was "just cleaning up the streets."

Interestingly, Sutcliffe also exhibited signs of being a Visionary serial killer, since he claimed he heard voices from God telling him to commit the atrocities he did.

What are some examples of a Hedonistic serial killer?

Hedonistic serial killing is actually a very broad category that can be broken down into three further subcategories:

- ✦ Lust - Kills for their own sexual satisfaction
- ✦ Thrill - Kills for the adrenaline rush
- ✦ Comfort - Kills for financial or other material gains.

Edmund Kemper is an ideal example of a Lust killer. Between 1972 and 1973, Kemper picked up a total of six female hitchhikers around Santa Cruz, California, then attacked, strangled, and dismembered them. Each of his kills gave Kemper sexual gratification—not just from the act of killing, but also from the act of postmortem mutilation. He is noted for his height of 6 feet 9 inches (2.06 m) and his intellect, possessing an IQ of 145. Most of his murders included necrophilia, with occasional incidents of rape.

California's most famous unidentified serial killer, the Zodiac, is the perfect example of a Hedonistic Thrill killer. The Zodiac reveled in the adrenaline rush he received from terrorizing the streets of San Francisco throughout the 1970s. Not only did the Zodiac murder couples in lovers' lanes throughout the city, but he also taunted the press and police with vile letters.

Female serial killers tend to fall into the Comfort killer category since very few of them are motivated by lust or power. Perhaps the most famous Comfort killer of all was Dorothea Puente, the landlady of a boarding house in Sacramento, California who drugged and killed her elderly tenants. Puente would then cash her victims' social security checks for financial gain. Puente's total count reached nine murders; she was convicted of three and the jury hung on the other six. Newspapers dubbed Puente the "Death House Landlady".

Interestingly, there is one infamous serial killer who combines elements of all three Hedonistic serial killer subcategories. Harold Shipman, a British GP, is considered to be one of the most prolific serial killers in modern history, with an estimated 250 victims. Shipman, considered to be one of the most prolific serial killers of all time, received both sexual and thrilling sensations from his murders, and in one case, forged one of his victim's wills to include himself.

What are some examples of a Power/Control serial killer?

Some of the most prolific serial killers of all time have been Power/Control serial killers since it's the most common serial killer type. Ted Bundy is perhaps the most archetypical

Power/Control serial killer; he craved domination over every aspect of his victims' lives. He would manipulate them, brutally attack them, sexually assault them, and discard their bodies in out-of-the-way locations. Bundy would also return to the crime scenes after death to violate his victims' corpses further still.

Other Power/Control serial killers include John Wayne Gacy, Dennis Rader (BTK), Gary Ridgway, Ian Brady, David Parker Ray, Andrei Chikatilo, and James DeAngelo (The East Area Rapist).

Did You Know?

- ⊕ Power/Control types are the most common form of serial killers
- ⊕ These types tend to harbor feelings of inadequacy
- ⊕ They often (but not always) have endured violent, abusive childhoods at the hands of their parents and elders
- ⊕ Power/Control killers even manipulate their victims after death, often through postmortem mutilation, sexual violation, or by keeping souvenirs of the crime.
- ⊕ Ted Bundy, one of the most infamous Power/Control serial killers, would take jewelry from his victims and give them to his girlfriend (who was blissfully unaware of their origins).

Can these serial killer types overlap?

Very much so. In most cases, it's only the Visionary serial killer that tends to stay firmly within one category. Other serial offenders often incorporate multiple types throughout their reigns, although they often retain one type as their "core" characteristic.

The Hedonistic serial killer regularly forays into Power/Control territory throughout their killing sprees, particularly Lust components. Those killers who derive sexual gratification from the act of murder often do so through domination and control, so these two types are closely intertwined.

Do any serial killers NOT fit into any of these categories?

Almost all serial killers fit into one or more of the categories above, even if their motive doesn't seem clear to those with a rational mind. However, there have been a handful of rare "motiveless" serial killers.

In 2007, two teenage killers from Russia, now dubbed the Dnepropetrovsk Maniacs, killed a total of 21 people in a single month. One of their murders, which saw the two boys bludgeon a man to death with a hammer, was filmed and uploaded to the Internet in 2008. To this day, no motive has ever been put forward. There were rumors that a wealthy benefactor was paying the boys to murder for his own personal amusement, but police found no evidence to corroborate such beliefs. Later, one of the investigators said they believed that the boys were simply murdering "as a hobby. To them, murder was like entertainment or hunting."

Another famous anomaly when it comes to motivation is British serial killer Robert Maudsley. Maudsley, also known as Hannibal Cannibal due to the fact he's kept in an underground glass cell similar to Hannibal Lecter in *The Silence of the Lambs*, did not seem to possess any motive for at least two of the murders he committed. In 1974, Maudsley garroted a local sex offender in London, England then handed himself into the authorities. Once inside prison, he killed three of his fellow inmates, including two people in one day. A guard later said that Maudsley would "get the urge to kill anyone who came near him." Due to his history of violence, when outside his cell he is escorted by at least four prison officers.

Who was the first ever serial killer?

The general consensus is that a man by the name of H.H. Holmes, a swindler and conman who built a "murder hotel" in Chicago to dispatch his victims in the 1890s, was the first ever serial killer. However, despite this common belief, we can trace the origins of serial killing back much further.

Gilles de Rais, a knight and commander in the Royal French Army in the early 1400s, is the earliest known serial killer in recorded history. Rais, who inherited great wealth and status in his teenage years, would order his generals to abduct young boys and girls between the ages of six and 18. These victims were then brought to Rais's secluded quarters, where he would then strip them naked, molest, torture, and murder them. He mostly slashed his victims' throats with a double-edged sword but would sometimes decapitate them. Postmortem, Rais would mutilate his victims' bodies further, removing and admiring their internal organs. Over a decade, Rais killed a minimum of 40 youngsters, with some sources stating the real number is closer to 100.

While Rais fits the typical psychopathology of a Hedonistic killer with Power/Control fantasies, historical differences and his high status make him incomparable to modern serial killers who act alone and take every effort to cover their tracks.

Many consider London's Jack the Ripper to be the typical blueprint of the modern-day serial killer. He attacked and killed five sex workers throughout the East End of London in 1888. However, only four years before 1884, a similar monster was at work in Austin, Texas. The perpetrator, now known as the "Servant Girl Annihilator," took the lives of at least eight victims over 12 months, eventually vanishing into the night in December 1885. The killer, who was never apprehended, snuck into the quarters of African American girls while they were sleeping and bludgeoned them to death with an axe. In some cases, he raped and mutilated his victims, and even inserted sharp implements into their ears. At the time, the African American community in Austin, Texas believed that the killer was using black magic to keep himself invisible.

What country has the most serial killers?

One country stands out far above the rest in terms of serial killers per capita, and that's the United States.

Between 1900 and 2016, the USA has had at least 3,204 serial killers to its name - a staggering number by any metric. Next to the USA is South Africa, which has endured 167 serial killers in the same time frame. That means that the USA has had just over 19 times as many serial killers as the next country on the list.

Why does every other country pale in comparison to the United States? Are there social and economic factors? Well, the truth may be a little more muddled than the US simply "having" more serial killers than any other country.

The United States is one of the most advanced countries in the world, both technologically and scientifically. Additionally, the US has many systems of interconnectivity, allowing states and localities to communicate effectively and share information. The United States may not have more serial killers than similar-sized countries but might simply just be more effective at catching them.

In less-developed but similar-sized countries like India or Russia, the number may be of similar scope to the USA, but their lack of efficient law enforcement techniques might keep this number much lower, at least officially. Not to mention that the United States is the fourth-largest country in the world by area, so it's naturally going to have more offenders, pro rata, than smaller countries.

Did You Know?

- The USA has both the highest number of recorded serial killers and the highest rate per capita (0.99% per every 100,000 people).
- California is the US state that has produced the most serial killers, boasting over 1,000 since 1900. During the 1970s, California was dubbed the "murder capital of the world."
- Canada has only seen 106 serial killers between 1900 and 2016, despite its landmass being 1.6% larger than the

United States. This puts its capita rate at 0.29% per 100,000 people.

- ✣ Iceland has one of the lowest crime rates in the world and has only ever produced one single recorded serial killer - Axlar-Björn Pétursson, in the 1500s.
- ✣ The Philippines also claims to have had only one serial killer in its history; a Catholic Priest who allegedly killed 57 people between 1816 and 1826.

Why doesn't the world see as many serial killers as it used to?

It's certainly true that the "golden age of serial killing" is long gone. Today, forensic and technological advancements have made it difficult for serial killers to thrive, and potential serial killers are often discovered before they have a chance to obtain serial status. DNA testing is now standard procedure for all homicide cases across the United States, and CCTV systems are now able to cover a much broader scope than what they could during the 1970s and 1980s.

So, while the serial killer mindset might exist in many potential offenders, law enforcement can intercept these killers before their victim counts reach the "serial" level. This isn't to say that serial killers don't exist in the modern age - law enforcement capabilities have just improved to the point we're better at catching them.

Are dictators or terrorists seen as serial killers?

The simple answer is no. Both of these types of crime fall under the banner of "political killing," which only shares similarities with serial killing in that innocent people often lose their lives. With dictators, terrorists, and arguably soldiers of war, there is usually a detachment between the killer and the victim. The mindset is not the same since none of them (or very few of them) kill for sexual gratification or an adrenaline rush.

Of course, there may be exceptions because (as we'll find out later) many psychopaths are drawn to the world of politics for thrill-seeking purposes.

What's the most common murder weapon for a serial killer?

When we picture the classic image of a serial killer, we tend to imagine hooded figures stalking shadowy backstreets, fingers curled around a gleaming steel blade. However, while knives are generally considered to be the serial killer's weapon of choice, stabbing actually comes in at a surprising third on the list.

A serial killer's most commonly used murder weapon is a pistol. This may seem like an unexpected revelation, especially as guns seem at odds with what the serial killer is trying to achieve: primal connection and an intimate experience of death. But guns allow the serial killer to gain full control of a victim despite the killer's physical limitations. Killers who aren't able to subdue victims with their bare hands often use guns because the threat of being shot often reduces victims into a submissive state, and for those killers who crave instant death, guns are the easiest option. Of the 10,000 or so recorded serial murders since 1900, shootings account for more than half of them.

After shooting, the second most common murder method is strangulation, accounting for 22% of serial killings since 1990. Stabbing comes in at number three, equaling around 15%.

Other methods of serial killing include bombing, drowning, poisoning, burning, axing, smothering, and vehicular homicide.

Did You Know?

- ⊕ While there have been many one-off instances of people using bizarre items to kill others (including socks, microwaves, shovels, scissors, chainsaws, and even toilet lids), most serial murderers stick with guns, knives, ropes, or their bare hands
- ⊕ Perhaps the most unique weapon to ever be used in a multi-homicide case was a samurai sword, used by Teodoro Baez to kill two people in Chicago in 1999
- ⊕ According to a Radford University study, serial killers with higher IQs prefer bombs and poison over guns and knives
- ⊕ Meanwhile, lower IQ serial killers tend to bludgeon or stab their victims.

What's the typical age and race of a serial killer?

The typical image of a serial killer is a mid-twenties to mid-thirties, white male, reasonably skinny, and not very attractive. The reality isn't too far off. Of serial killers caught in the United States, 92.3% are male. However, only 27% are in their mid-twenties to mid-thirties. Even more surprisingly, only 52.1% of US serial killers are white.

In fact, 40.3% of serial killers are black, while 7% are Hispanic. Native Americans and Asian serial killers make up 1% each. For male serial killers, the average age of first committing murder is 27.5. For women, the average age of their first kill is 32.

What is the "modus operandi"?

If you've watched any crime procedural, you've probably heard the term "modus operandi," before, or "M.O." for short. Modus operandi translates from Latin as "method of operation." It's a crucial part of the investigative process as it explains exactly how an offender approached and committed their particular crimes. The textbook definition is:

"Modus Operandi, or M.O., refers to those behaviors committed during an offense that serve to ensure its completion while also protecting the perpetrator's identity and facilitating escaping following the offense. M.O. accounts for how an offender commits his crimes. It is what the offender does and has to do to commit his crimes."

Does a serial killer's M.O. stay the same all the time?

Over a long enough timeline, the modus operandi is the one aspect of the crime that is most likely to change and evolve (or in some cases, devolve). Serial killers tend to hone their craft as they rack up their body counts.

For example, Ted Bundy's modus operandi started as peeping through windows at women he admired, which then progressed into stalking his prey and blitz-attacking them from behind.

Finally, Bundy's M.O. changed again when he included aspects of necrophilia in his crimes. The M.O. is usually a process of trial and error. If one thing doesn't work during one crime, the offender may change it, adapt it, or omit it during the next.

Richard Ramirez - the Night Stalker - broke into homes through open windows or unlocked doors. However, as he became more confident in his abilities, he began picking locks and breaking windows to obtain access to the homes he wanted.

Very few M.O.s remain identical throughout a serial killer's career. Slight variations will always be included, even if the end result (torture, rape, sodomy, murder) is always the same. The end goal is complete satisfaction and complete control of what is happening; therefore, the modus operandi will evolve as such.

What are a "signature" and a "ritual"?

The signature is the component of the crime that addresses the killer's personal fantasies. The signature goes beyond what is necessary for the crime to be committed. It addresses the murderer's emotional and psychological needs. Unlike the M.O., the signature will rarely, if ever, change.

A signature will also display the offender's primary motive for carrying out the murder. For example, if a victim has been tortured or mutilated then sexual sadism would be the signature, which in turn provides the motivation. If a victim has their possessions stolen following their murder, the signature would be robbery.

While often used interchangeably with the term signature, the concept of a "ritual" is generally reserved for when there is a clear definition between M.O. and signature. Alternatively, it is also used when the offender displays ritualistic behavior as opposed to compulsive behavior.

For example, serial killers may go through a series of steps to stage their crime scene to address their specific fantasies. They may pose their victim in a particular position, remove their valuables, leave a "calling card", carry out post-mortem mutilation, kill victims in a specific order (Richard Ramirez always targeted the male first), or a combination of the above. In such cases, due to the methodological approach employed by the killer, this would be termed as more ritualistic than merely a signature.

THE PSYCHOPATHIC MIND

Serial killers and psychopathy go hand in hand. Quite often, the term "psychopath" is used as a catch-all term when referring to murderers, since after all, an offender must be suffering some kind of mental ailment to commit the kinds of atrocities we're talking about. However, the psychopathic mind is actually much broader and more complex than people realize, and surprisingly, not all serial killers can be officially labeled as psychopaths.

What is a psychopath, exactly?

The term "psychopath" is often used to describe a wide range of personalities, usually aggressive and remorseless ones. However, psychopathy is actually a clinical term with strict guidelines surrounding its definition.

Psychopathy is an antisocial personality disorder typified by several common traits, including:

- ✠ Antisocial behavior
- ✠ Superficial charm
- ✠ Lack of emotion

- ⊕ Lack of guilt
- ⊕ Narcissism
- ⊕ Impulsivity
- ⊕ Lack of empathy
- ⊕ Parasitic lifestyle
- ⊕ Poor behavioral controls

These traits might sound quite common amongst the general population, and indeed, most people may exhibit one or two of them regularly. However, these people would not be considered psychopaths. The most accurate analogy to explain psychopathy is to think of the disorder as a mixing desk, with each of the traits an individual dial. If each dial is raised above a certain level, only then should that person be labeled a psychopath.

Around 29% of the entire population exhibit one or more of these traits regularly, but only 0.6% of the population can be designated as psychopaths. While many people possess these traits, only those that display them in everyday behavior can truly be considered psychopathic.

What's the difference between a psychopathic and a sociopathic serial killer?

The terms "psychopath" and "sociopath" are often used interchangeably, especially when referring to the world's most heinous serial killers. However, there are clinical differences between the two, although it's important to keep in mind that these psychological terms are constantly evolving and changing. While someone might refer to a particular serial killer as a psychopath or sociopath, they're not always describing them in the way we'll discuss in a second.

The core difference between psychopathic and sociopathic serial killers is that psychopaths tend to be more "organized," while sociopaths are considered "disorganized." For example, psychopathic serial killers might possess/exhibit the following:

- Emotionally controlled and methodical
- Of average or above-average intelligence
- Socially competent, persuasive, and manipulative
- Often a skilled worker or self-employed
- Sexually adequate
- Subject to minimal discipline as a child
- Moderate use of alcohol before/after a crime
- Takes an interest in the media reports about their crimes
- Often married, divorced, or has children
- Likely to return to the scene of the crime
- Carries out their crimes in a familiar area
- Purposely personalizes and terrorizes the victim to experience a higher layer of power
- Takes additional effort to remove all forensic evidence from the crime scene
- Takes trophies from their victims.

Contrastingly, a sociopathic serial killer might possess/exhibit the following:

- Impulsive, prone to violent outbursts
- Below average intelligence
- Unskilled worker
- Often sexually inadequate

- ✦ Harsh, abusive upbringing
- ✦ Uses alcohol before committing murder
- ✦ Lives alone
- ✦ Depersonalizes their victims to see them as objects to reduce surges of conscience
- ✦ Kills during windows of opportunity
- ✦ Often doesn't conceal the victim's body post-murder
- ✦ Does not fully realize the severity of their actions.

Who was a typical psychopathic serial killer?

Dennis Rader, aka BTK, was the archetypical psychopathic serial killer. Rader was a respected family man and member of his community in Wichita, Kansas. However, he lived a double life as a homicidal serial killer, claiming ten lives between 1974 and 1991.

Rader would stalk his victims for a considerable time before striking, usually learning their schedules. When the time came, he would bring along all the tools he needed to break into someone's home and murder them: screwdriver, rope, duct tape. He also cut some of his victims' phone lines before entering their homes to stop them from calling for help.

Following each murder, Rader would take trophies from his victims, often women's underwear. He then taunted the press and police with vile letters, one of them asking, "How many do I have to kill before I get a name in the paper or some national recognition?" As well as deriving sexual satisfaction from his crimes, Rader was also obsessed with celebrity status.

Who's the best example of a sociopathic serial killer?

The most heinous female serial killer of all time, Aileen Wuornos, exhibited classic sociopathic behavior during her murder spree. Wuornos was a sex worker who trawled Florida highways, and between 1989 and 1990, she shot and killed six men.

The men that Wuornos killed had all enlisted her services as an escort at the time of their deaths. Wuornos claimed that the men turned aggressive once they were in her private company (although this portion of Wuornos's tale is still debated), and Wuornos simply acted out against them in rage. Once she'd killed her victims, Wuornos would steal and pawn their possessions. She discarded their bodies in wooded areas around Florida but made little effort to conceal them. Upon being tested in prison, Aileen Wuornos was found to have an IQ of only 81.

Did You Know?

- Jack the Ripper, one of the first serial killers to capture the public imagination, was considered to be a disorganized sociopath
- Ted Bundy, generally considered to be the gold standard of psychopaths, exhibited high levels of sociopathy, particularly in his latter murders
- Sociopathic serial killers tend to blitz-attack their victims to gain immediate control of the situation.

And what's a "psychotic?"

Psychotic serial killers often overlap with the "disorganized" category of offender, but psychotics tend to be marred by extreme mental illness that greatly distorts their worldview. They almost always fall into the Visionary category of a serial killer as we mentioned earlier, usually blaming their actions on an external force that compels them to commit murder.

These types of killers tend to be a lot more random and chaotic than their psychopathic counterparts. They will more likely target strangers and carry out attacks in violent bursts. They will often take great risks and leave behind a great deal of evidence, rarely taking the time (or having the mental foresight) to clean up their crime scenes or dispose of their victims' bodies in isolated locations.

Are there "mixed" serial killers?

Since "organized," "disorganized," and "psychotic" are quite broad terms, not all serial killers fit neatly into one category or the other. There are numerous factors that can influence a serial killer's eventual designation, including intelligence, status, self-awareness, use of intoxicants, circumstantial issues, and more. Therefore, some of the typical traits can crossover.

Jeffrey Dahmer is often considered a "mixed" offender, as his crimes displayed symptoms of organization, disorganization, and indeed psychotic behavior. Dahmer would target gay men around his neighborhood in Milwaukee, Wisconsin, luring them back to his apartment under the pretext of having sex with them. There, he would intoxicate them and restrain them, then he would kill and dismember their corpses. On one occasion, one of Dahmer's victims managed to escape his apartment and even flagged down passing police officers, but Dahmer was able to convince these officers to let the man go. Dahmer then took the man back to his apartment and killed him.

This all shows signs of incredible organization and capability, but Dahmer was often so drunk during his murders that he claimed not to remember them. He worked a low-level, unskilled job, lived alone, and rarely took the necessary precautions to cover his tracks. He would also dismember his victims to extreme levels, preserving their body parts in jars around his apartment.

Are all serial killers psychopaths?

This question has been the subject of much debate over the decades, and the consensus is that no, not all serial killers can officially be termed as psychopaths. There is, of course, a very high correlation between psychopathy and serial killing, and the majority of serial killers undoubtedly suffer from one or more antisocial personality disorders. However, terming it simply as psychopathy is misleading.

According to a 2001 study by Columbia University professor Michael H. Stone:

- ⊕ 86.5% of serial killers met the PCL-R (psychopathy checklist) criteria for psychopathy. An additional 9.0% had traits of psychopathy.
- ⊕ 87.5% of serial killers met the DSM-III (The Diagnostic and Statistical Manual of Mental Disorders) criteria for sadistic

personality disorder. An additional 1.5% had traits of sadistic personality disorder.

+ Half of the serial killers met the DSM-IV criteria for schizoid personality disorder. An additional 4.0% had traits of schizoid personality disorder.

What are the common psychopathic traits?

Psychopathic traits can take a wide variety of forms, but they can generally be condensed to a few select traits. The most common psychopathic traits are:

+ Aggressive behavior
+ Prone to violent outbursts
+ Superficial charm and charisma
+ Tendency to lie
+ Unable to distinguish between right and wrong
+ Difficulty showing remorse or empathy
+ Lack of regard for safety and responsibility
+ Behavior that conflicts with societal norms
+ Violating the rights of others
+ Parasitic living
+ Manipulating or purposely hurting others
+ Regular problems with the law
+ Impulsivity and failure to plan
+ Boredom and thrill-seeking behavior
+ No concern for consequences.

What's the MacDonald Triad?

The MacDonald Triad, colloquially termed the "Triad of Evil," is a series of factors, the presence of any two of which are considered to indicate a person might possess violent tendencies. The theory was put forward by psychiatrist J.M. MacDonald in 1963.

The idea is that these three factors can suggest that a child might grow up to commit violent acts, and quite often, these three factors are found amongst serial killers. These factors are:

- ✦ Animal cruelty
- ✦ Committing acts of arson
- ✦ Regularly wetting the bed.

Animal cruelty suggests that the child is looking to take control of their environment or indulge their penchant for power play. MacDonald believed that the child may have been exposed to abuse by authoritative adults, to which the child couldn't retaliate. Therefore, the child vents their frustrations out on something weaker.

MacDonald believed that acts of arson were ways for children to unload their feelings of helplessness and aggression, all within the confines of a "detached" crime. Children with these tendencies would perhaps relish the chaos that fire would provide while providing visible consequences that would satiate their need for havoc.

Bedwetting, also known as enuresis, was considered by MacDonald to be linked with similar feelings of humiliation that also invoked the other traits in the triad. Additionally, MacDonald considered bedwetting to be a symptom of a lack of impulse control, something that serial killers possess in abundance. (Note: *Enuresis is "unintentional bed-wetting during sleep, persistent after the age of five". The bed-wetting must continue twice a week for at least three consecutive months.*)

Is the MacDonald Triad accurate?

While the MacDonald Triad is generally considered to be the blueprint for diagnosing potential violent tendencies in children, it has been subject to closer scrutiny since its inception. In 1966, an independent study found that of 88 incarcerated violent criminals, 87 of them possessed at least two of the traits during childhood. In 2004, a further study found an even stronger link between animal cruelty and violence toward humans.

However, in 2018, a study found that a significant percentage of modern violent criminals did not possess two or more of the traits in the MacDonald Triad as children. Instead, the researchers concluded that, rather than being an indication of future violent behavior, the MacDonald Triad suggested that the child suffered an abusive home environment, but this might not lead to criminal activities as an adult.

Do all psychopaths possess the desire to murder?

No, not at all. There are many functioning psychopaths out there right now living perfectly ordinary and peaceful lives who have no desire to hurt others. Psychopaths are complex creatures, just like any neurotypical individual, and their motivations and personalities can greatly vary.

With this said, many of these "functioning" psychopaths do possess the same traits listed above, in that they lack remorse and may exhibit superficial charm to achieve their goals. But most people, psychopathic or not, do not have any desire to murder anyone.

How many people are psychopaths?

It's difficult to make an accurate analysis of just how many psychopaths are walking the earth, but it's estimated that between 0.75%–1% of people possess psychopathic tendencies. There are certain areas where psychopathy is more common, particularly in high-populated cities as psychopaths are often attracted to the business world.

It's also estimated that correctional facilities around the United States are made up of 25% psychopaths.

Can psychopathy be used for good?

Very much so. Psychopaths make for excellent leaders in the business world, and due to their lack of emotion, they thrive in high-stress, high-risk occupations. Psychopaths are assertive. They don't waste time. They don't beat themselves up if things go wrong and they're constantly striving for the next achievement. For these reasons, psychopaths tend to excel in certain industries (more on this in a later chapter). The medical and business worlds, law enforcement, and militaries all over the world are often brimming with those who display psychopathic tendencies.

According to Kevin Dutton, author of *The Wisdom of Psychopaths* (2012), there are many psychopaths permeating the world of showbusiness too. Dutton even claims that rock star Bruce Dickinson, singer for the legendary band Iron Maiden and commercial airline pilot, is actually a "good" psychopath with the ability to keep himself cool in the face of mounting stress and pressure.

Can you recognize a psychopath by looking at them?

It's considered impossible to "see" a psychopath, at least with a single glance. Not only do psychopaths possess the same visual traits as neurotypical people, but psychopaths are also masters of camouflage. They've spent their entire lives learning how to adapt to social expectations, even adjusting their surface behavior accordingly to blend in with the masses.

However, there is one area that might betray a psychopath's true intentions, and that's their eyes.

Some people may be familiar with the famous "psychopath eyes": the cold stare that portrays no emotion even in the face of adversity, and for many years, this was considered a myth. However, new scientific findings have discovered there might be some truth behind the legend.

The eyes are a cornerstone of body language and nonverbal signaling. This includes the directions we look when asked to recall information, how long we're able to hold someone else's gaze, how we narrow and widen them when presented with information, and so forth.

Additionally, our pupils tend to dilate when we see something that upsets, offends, or disturbs us, usually brought on by our biological "fight or flight" response. They also dilate if something exhilarates us - one of the reasons that veteran card players check their opponents' eyes to see if they might have a good hand.

But with psychopaths, this pupil dilation is rarely present, especially when presented with threatening or potentially stressful situations. Given their lack of emotion, they don't respond to these kinds of situations the way ordinary people would, so if you want to discern whether someone is a psychopath, take note of their pupils.

Do psychopaths know they're psychopaths?

Mostly, yes. Psychopaths are very aware that something is wrong with them, but since psychopaths don't dwell on their thoughts too much, most never go above this level. Since all psychopaths have felt the same way since birth, they go a long time without realizing that other people don't possess the same lack of emotion as they do.

One of the key reasons that psychopaths don't realize their situation is that psychopathy is often depicted in media as quite different to reality. While the mainstream image is that psychopaths possess zero emotional capabilities whatsoever, this isn't true in the reality. Psychopaths *do* possess an ounce of emotional awareness, it's just very dulled down. Therefore, a psychopath might not believe themselves to be one because they're aware of their own feelings, while wrongly believing that psychopaths are pure, emotionless monsters.

Are psychopathic serial killers born or made?

One of the oldest questions in criminal psychology concerns whether serial killers are born or made - nature versus nurture. The truth, as anticlimactic as it may be, lies somewhere in the middle.

Psychopaths are undoubtedly born with their condition. No amount of medical or therapeutic intervention can stop a psychopath from harboring cravings for power and domination. It's a part of their identity from the moment they become self-aware. Of course, as we mentioned earlier, the degree to which psychopaths possess these traits varies widely.

However, not every psychopath goes on to become a cold-blooded murderer. Some go on to have fruitful, pleasant lives without ever harming another soul. Therefore, there must be other factors at play that transform a psychopath into a serial killer.

One such factor is childhood abuse. A large majority of serial killers experienced violent upbringings, be it at the hands of their parents, siblings, and authoritative adults. This then distorts the psychopath's outlook on other human beings further still and instills a deep resentment that they might spend the rest of their lives trying to undo. It seems that a genetic predisposition toward violence and an abusive childhood is the most common recipe to transform a psychopath into a murderer.

Are serial killing psychopaths legally insane?

No. Very few psychopathic serial killers are officially labeled "insane." Insanity is a broad term that has no strict psychiatric classification. It's a legal term that changes between countries, states, and localities, but the general legal definition is: "a mental illness of such a severe nature that a person cannot distinguish fantasy from reality, cannot conduct her/his affairs due to psychosis, or is subject to uncontrollable impulsive behavior."

While *some* serial killers do fit the insanity definition, most psycho and sociopaths are fully aware of their actions but simply have no concern for the consequences. For this reason, psychopathic and sociopathic serial killers cannot be termed insane, despite many of them possessing abnormal thought patterns.

The "insanity defense" has become a popular trope in modern times, with many offenders attempting to downplay their murderous activities and receive less strict penalties through reason of insanity. However, despite this common ploy, very few serial killers are ever found legally insane.

Did You Know?

- The only serial killer who has ever successfully pleaded insanity was Ed Gein in 1968
- Albert Fish, a man who claimed to have killed over 100 children and heard voices from God, pleaded insanity in 1935 but was found sane and sentenced to death
- Jeffrey Dahmer also pleaded insanity but was found to be in full control of his mental faculties
- Other serial killers that have pleaded insanity include Kenneth Bianchi, Andrea Yates, Anthony Sowell, Peter Sutcliffe, and John Wayne Gacy,

Is Jacob's Syndrome related to psychopathy in serial killers?

Jacob's Syndrome is a rare genetic condition in which a male receives an extra Y chromosome from their father (resulting in an XYY chromosome make-up). This additional Y chromosome causes the body to produce excessive amounts of estrogen, which was found to be the case with serial killers Bobby Joe Long and Richard Speck. This interesting variable then prompted discussion as to whether it might be a seed that later caused the two criminals to commit murder, the belief being that an additional Y chromosome could make males more prone to violence.

It has since become something of a myth, and scientific data has proven that males with an extra Y chromosome are not genetically predisposed to more violent behavior than males who do not possess the same abnormality. The only tangible link is that the additional chromosome may create embarrassing effects for the male, such as more acne, increased breast size, and a higher-pitched voice, which may serve as a source of humiliation that could then be transposed into resentment.

Is there a "cure" for psychopathy?

No, there is no cure for psychopathy, at least not in the form of medical intervention. It is a personality disorder, not a mental illness, and therefore cannot be rectified through the same means one might treat mental ailments.

But while psychopathy cannot be "cured," it can be controlled through various means, particularly if the psychopath is imprisoned. The most efficient way to control a psychopath's behavior is through reward-based means, such as offering them their favorite foods or media if they behave accordingly. Negative treatment of psychopaths rarely produces results since psychopaths aren't concerned with consequences, pain, or discomfort. So, the bottom line is that people who possess psychopathic traits will never change.

MOTIVATIONS:
WHAT DRIVES
A SERIAL KILLER?

While it might not make sense to any rational mind, all serial killers have a reason for doing what they do, however absurd and surreal this reason might sound. Sometimes, it can be as simple as sexual gratification or a desire to control another human being. Other motivations can be unique, unbelievable, and even downright bizarre. Motivations are the backbone of serial killing since they are what prompt these monsters to commit such horrific acts.

What's the strangest serial killer motivation of all time?

Herbert Mullin, a Californian serial killer who killed 13 people between 1972 and 1973, did so because he believed that it would prevent earthquakes from hitting his hometown. Mullin falls firmly into the "psychotic" bracket of serial killers, acting out because of a misplaced belief that warped his perception of reality.

Mullin was born on April 16, 1947, on the anniversary of the famous 1906 earthquake. This little detail, combined with excessive drugs and Mullin's already-twisted outlook on life, greatly affected Mullin once he reached his adult years.

This was certainly one of the more bizarre serial killer motivations, but of course, everything made sense in Mullin's distorted mind.

Did You Know?

- Mullin first killed a homeless man with a baseball bat, believing the man was Jonah from the Bible who had sent Mullin the telepathic message - "kill me so others will be saved"
- One of Mullin's victims, a 24-year-old woman, was not initially attributed to Mullin because authorities believed it was the work of another serial killer operating at the same time - Edmund Kemper
- Herbert Mullin had no particular victimology, killing both men and women, young and old
- There were indeed no earthquakes during Mullin's entire killing spree, but bizarrely, one hit California within weeks of his arrest!

Are the motivations of male killers different from female killers?

For the most part, men and women claim very different motivations when it comes to serial killing. While men tend to kill for power, domination, and sexual gratification, women tend to kill for personal gain. As mentioned, a few chapters previous, the majority of women are Comfort killers.

When a woman kills, there is usually an identifiable reason and one that often benefits the woman's life in some way. Financial gain is a huge motivator for female serial killers, as is "removing" an unnecessary burden from their life, be it a foe or an unwanted husband.

Female serial killers also differ when it comes to killing methods. While men are more likely to use guns or knives, females keep things much more low-key. Poisoning is the most common method utilized by female serial killers, followed closely by stabbing and then suffocation. Additionally, women are much more likely to kill someone they know than a stranger. The desire for lust fulfillment is rarely present in female killers, although there are a handful of exceptions (Rose West, Joanna Dennehy, Karla Homolka).

On the flip side, and somewhat disturbingly, women are also more likely to kill children than men are.

What British serial killer was motivated by loneliness?

Dennis Nilsen was an isolated, socially stunted Scotsman from Aberdeenshire whose motivation for killing 12 men was loneliness. Between 1978 and 1983, Nilsen lured young gay men back to his London apartment, and then strangled or drowned them. Afterwards, Nilsen would then bathe and dress up the corpses of his victims, and sexually violate them, before dissecting and disposing of the remains by burning them in a bonfire or flushing them down a toilet.

Upon his arrest, Nilsen claimed that he "killed for company," and that the important part of the process was not the killing, but "cohabitation" he relished once the deed was done. He later claimed in a prison statement:

> *"When under the pressure of work and extreme pain of social loneliness and utter misery, I am drawn compulsively to a means of temporary escape from reality. When I take alcohol, I see myself drawn along and moved out of my isolated, prison flat. I bring [with me] people who are not always allowed to leave because I want them to share my experiences and high feeling."*

Due to his similar modus operandi and motivation, Dennis Nilsen is often referred to as the British Jeffrey Dahmer.

What shooter killed because she "didn't like Mondays?"

Brenda Spencer not only has one of the most unbelievable motivations in serial killing history, but she was also America's first-ever female school shooter.

In January 1979, Brenda Spencer, a troubled child from San Diego, California, fired 36 rounds out of her home window at children waiting outside the gates to Grover Cleveland Elementary School. Spencer was only 17 years old at the time of the shooting that killed the principal and a custodian. Eight children and police officer Robert Robb were injured.

Upon being arrested, Spencer told police that she did it because "she didn't like Mondays" and that shooting people would "liven up the day." The incident inspired the famous Boomtown Rats song 'I Don't Like Mondays.'

Who was the infamous grave robber who stole corpses to make a woman's dress out of their skin?

Perhaps one of the famous serial killers of all time, Ed Gein, also had one of the strangest motivations for committing the vile acts that he did. Ed Gein was something of a momma's boy, doting on his devout Christian mother from the day he was born. When she passed away, Gein went to disturbing levels to resurrect her memory.

Gein would haunt the graveyards of Plainfield, Wisconsin, digging up the graves of recently deceased old women. He would then take the corpses back to his farmhouse and dissect them, planning to create a skinsuit that he would wear to roleplay the part of his dead mother.

But when corpses weren't enough, Gein turned to live women. He shot two women in his local town, took them home, and did the same again. When police investigated Gein's home, they found an assortment of bizarre creations made from human skin and bone.

Did You Know?

- Despite being one of the most infamous serial killers of all time, Ed Gein did not fit the FBI definition of a serial killer for many years due to only having claimed two victims
- As well as killing two women, police also suspected Gein was involved in the death of his own brother
- Until the police raided the Gein home in 1957, no one had stepped foot in the bedroom of Ed Gein's mother for 12 years

- Ed Gein is the only American serial killer to successfully plead insanity
- During Ed Gein's interrogation, the arresting sheriff was so furious at Gein for what he'd done that he violently attacked Gein, causing Gein's initial confession to be inadmissible due to head trauma

What Indian serial killer believed that he could become a mystic healer after killing 70 women?

Ahmad Suradji was a serial killer from India who certainly possesses one of the strangest motivations of all time, as well as having an abnormally high body count.

Suradji's reign of terror lasted a total of 11 years between 1986 and 1997. Suradji was a professional "dukun," which is a form of a shaman in India believed to possess magical abilities. Women would visit Suradji hoping to use his wisdom to improve their lives. Suradji would take these women out into a sugarcane field and bury them up to their waist, claiming it was all part of a ritual to make them more beautiful and wealthier.

Once they were half-buried, Suradji strangled the women and then, bizarrely, drank their saliva. After police finally became aware of Suradji's activities, Suradji claimed that his father's ghost had visited him in a dream and demanded he drank the saliva of 70 women to become a mystic healer.

When police dug up the sugarcane field, they found the decomposing remains of 42 women. Suradji's three wives (who were also sisters) were also arrested for assisting Suradji in his numerous murders.

Who killed because they believed their victims were poisoning him with witchcraft?

Juan Covington is a serial killer from Pennsylvania who claimed that his victims were trying to telepathically poison him.

Covington had a long history of mental illness, brought on in his twenties when his father passed away. Covington then began acting strange, and in 1998, he shot a local Baptist Pastor for seemingly no clear reason. Seven years later, in 2005, he shot a random man in the street, again with no clear motive.

The same year, Covington shot and killed Patricia McDermott, a radiographer for Pennsylvania Hospital. CCTV footage led police to Juan Covington, who confessed with little provocation. Covington, a worker at the same hospital as McDermott, claimed that he killed her because she was trying to poison him with x-rays. Amazingly, Covington then confessed to the two previous murders, stating both men had been trying to poison him with witchcraft.

What Uber driver-turned spree killer killed because he claimed the Devil spoke to him through his Uber app?

On a single night in February 2016, six people were killed in Kalamazoo County, Michigan by a man named Jason Dalton. Dalton opened fire in seemingly random locations around the city: an apartment complex, outside a restaurant, and in a car dealership.

When police arrested Dalton - a man with no prior history of mental illness - he claimed that his Uber mobile app had driven him to commit the mass shootings. Dalton said that the Uber symbol reminded him of the sigil of the Order of the Eastern Star (a Masonic Fraternity) and that it took control of his entire body. He said that when he pushed the app on his phone, a new app popped up and the Devil spoke directly to him through the screen. Apparently, his app switched from black to red, and that's when the Devil was in control. He told police:

> "I just tapped it and then there was like a devil head that popped up. It was some sort of like horned, horned head like a cow head or something. When I tapped that, it said that I could say whatever I wanted to. There would be no repercussions. When it's in that black mode, it literally has control of you. It would do a little blink at me. The minute that the app went from black to red, it had my presence."

What's the most mundane motive a serial killer has had?

In Alaska in 1979, police discovered the decomposed remains of a man along the Alaskan highway. The victim, whose identity has never been verified, was nicknamed One-Eyed Jack due to allegedly having lost an eye in a logging accident.

While One-Eyed Jack's killer was tracked down shortly after police found the body, the killer's identity has never been made public. For what reason remains unknown. All that's known is that One-Eyed Jack had been hitchhiking from Boise, Idaho, and ended up in Alaska with the man who eventually became his killer.

When police asked the killer why he murdered One-Eyed Jack and discarded his corpse along the highway, the killer responded,

"He was getting on my nerves." No other explanation was given, and the identity of this nonchalant killer remains a mystery.

What Japanese killer claimed his own fictional creation, the Rat Man, commanded him to kill?

Tsutomu Miyazaki, also known as the Otaku Killer, was one of Japan's most heinous and disturbing serial killers. Between 1988 and 1989, Miyazaki took the lives of four young girls throughout his native Tokyo, abducting, strangling, and then dismembering them.

Miyazaki was something of a loner, spending most of his time obsessing over videotapes in his bedroom. In his teenage years, he developed an unhealthy relationship with sex and pornography, particularly obsessing over girls' hands as Miyazaki himself had a mild hand deformity.

He would mutilate his victims' bodies, sometimes drinking their blood and eating their flesh once the dismemberment was complete. He paid close attention to the girls' hands and limbs, even stashing some of them away in his cupboard at home. Police apprehended Miyazaki in 1989, and during his trial, he blamed his actions on "the Rat Man," a fictional creature of his own making that allegedly took control of his body and mind during his crimes.

Bizarrely, police did indeed find depictions of this strange creature in Miyazaki's notebooks dating back to his childhood.

Why did the Russian serial killer Alexander Pichushkin only aspire to kill a certain number of victims?

Alexander Pichushkin's goal was to kill 64 people - just enough people to fill an entire chessboard, and to beat the body count of his idol, fellow serial killer Andrei Chikatilo.

Pichushkin grew up in Soviet Russia in the 1970s and 1980s, and from a young age developed a deep obsession with the game of chess. In his teenage years, Pichushkin began tormenting young boys, videoing them in private and using the videos to blackmail them.

In 1992, Pichushkin stepped into the realm of murder in a spree that lasted until 2006. He would mostly target homeless men, but he sometimes targeted women and children too. He would lure them to an isolated area of a nearby forest and then bludgeon them to death with a hammer. At first, he began disposing of his victims' remains down a well but later left them open to the elements.

Did You Know?

- Alexander Pichushkin kept a notebook in his pocket with a small chessboard sketched inside. Each square was filled in with a date, correlating to his murders.
- At the time of his arrest, Pichushkin had filled in 61 squares – only three short of his goal.
- Pichushkin is an extremely rare type of serial killer in that his body count had a maximum limit.

♦ Only one other serial killer claimed to have a victim count limit. British serial killer Stephen Griffiths wanted to kill 14 women to be "one higher than the Yorkshire Ripper."

What New York nurse disguised his serial killing as heroism?

Richard Angelo, aka, the Angel of Death, was a nurse who poisoned six hospital patients in 1987. The reason? He suffered from a complex known as Hero's Syndrome.

After getting a job as an emergency medical technician in Long Island, New York in 1987, Angelo became increasingly depressed at the lack of praise he was receiving from his fellow coworkers. Therefore, Angelo devised a method to look like a hero and show off his medical expertise.

Angelo began poisoning patients around the hospital with a combination of paralytic drugs. He would lace their IV tubes with the substances, and then once the patients began showing signs of distress, Angelo would arrive on the scene and "save" them.

Unfortunately, not only did several of Angelo's experiments fail and ended up killing the patients, but one of his victims actually caught him lacing his IV tube with drugs. In a police statement, Angelo later claimed:

"I wanted to create a situation where I would cause the patient to have some respiratory distress or some problem, and through my intervention or suggested intervention or whatever, come out looking like I knew what I was doing. I had no confidence in myself. I felt very inadequate."

What bizarre serial killer tried to "steal" his victims' voices?

Edward Leonski was a boxer, bodybuilder, and US soldier who had a strange obsession with women's voices. While on military duty in Melbourne, Australia in 1942, Leonski strangled three women, eventually cementing his moniker as the Brownout Strangler.

Leonski had something of a reputation amongst his fellow soldiers. He was a troubled young man who drank to oblivion regularly. He was a show-off and a womanizer. As a child, Leonski was exposed to regular domestic violence from his father, but his ailments were then soothed by his mother's sweet singing voice which sent him to sleep.

This fond memory then grimly echoed in Leonski's later years. By night, Leonski would target lone women on the streets of Melbourne, strangling them and leaving their bodies for the morning crowd to stumble upon. He killed three women in 15 days.

Leonski was quickly apprehended and later confessed his motive for the killings, saying that he held a sinister fascination with female voices, particularly when they were singing. Indeed, one of Leonski's victims had been a professional bar singer. Leonski claimed he wanted to keep his victims' voices for himself.

What serial killing duo wanted to kill one woman of every teenage age?

Roy Norris and Lawrence Bittaker, more famously known as the Toolbox Killers, were two of the most depraved and sadistic serial killers of all time. While cruelty and torture were their primary motivation for killing, Bittaker and Norris endeavored to complete a "collection." They wanted to kill one girl for every age between 13 and 19.

Bittaker and Norris first became acquainted in prison in 1977, then once both were released, they teamed up and began cruising around southern California in 1979, planning to abduct and torture women.

They would trick girls into hitchhiking with them or simply snatch them off the streets into their van they nicknamed the "Murder Mack." Once inside, Bittaker and Norris would restrain and gag the victims, then sexually assault and torture them for several hours. They would mostly use hand tools to carry out these horrific acts, eventually killing their victims via strangulation or with icepicks through their brains.

As a killing duo, Bittaker and Norris took the lives of five young women, never achieving their goal of killing one girl of every teenage age. The pair would often record their torture sessions with pictures and audio tapes.

Did You Know?

- ⊕ A brief section of the tape recording of the Toolbox Killer's final murder was played in court, causing many of the people present to flee the room in horror.
- ⊕ The same tape is used as part of FBI training for recruits to desensitize them to human violence.
- ⊕ Jonathan Demme, director of the hit film *The Silence of the Lambs*, was given access to the tape for research for the

film. He described it as the most disturbing thing he'd ever heard.

⊕ The tape has never been publicly released, although a (very disturbing) written transcript is available.

What female serial murderer killed to support her shopping addiction?

Over four weeks in 1994, American serial killer Dana Sue Gray killed three women for the sole reason of getting her fix of retail therapy.

Dana Sue Gray was in financial trouble. She was unemployed and had built up a mountain of debt. So, desperate for money, Gray went to extreme lengths to fix her issues. She began murdering people for money. She strangled three women around Southern California and, barely an hour after their deaths, used their credit cards to go on wild spending sprees.

Gray's final intended victim - an antique store worker - survived her attack and was able to provide investigators with a description of Gray.

What serial killer murdered women because of his shoe fetish?

Jerry Brudos, aka the Shoe Fetish Slayer, was a serial killer and necrophile from Webster, South Dakota. Brudos was abused by his mother from an early age because she wanted to give birth to a girl. At five years old, Jerry's obsession with women's shoes began when he found a pair of high heels in a junkyard. The following year, Brudos was caught trying to steal his first-grade teacher's shoes.

By his teenage years, Brudos was already in and out of mental hospitals around his home state. He abducted his first woman aged only 17, threatening to kill her if she didn't do as he commanded. He was promptly caught and sent to another mental hospital where he was diagnosed with schizophrenia and extreme misogyny.

Brudos' killing spree began in 1968. He first lured a woman selling encyclopedias into his home and killed her, then abducted a stranded woman on the side of a highway. He then began abducting women off the street, taking them to his home and strangling them. After their deaths, Brudos would have intercourse with the dead bodies and then take trophies in the form of shoes and amputated body parts. Then he'd weigh their bodies down with mechanical parts and dump them in rivers around South Dakota.

KILLING IS MY BUSINESS: SERIAL KILLERS AND JOBS

Serial killers only spend a fraction of their lives actually killing, so what do they do for the rest of their time? Like everyone else in society, they go to work. We might imagine serial killers as unemployed loners or office drones are driven to insanity by their mundane work, but the truth is that serial killers work in a wide variety of niches, industries, and occupations. In fact, some even hold high-status positions, and of course, some even use their occupations to their advantage.

What's the most common job type for a serial killer?

The cold truth is that serial killers can be found across a wide range of industries, services, and businesses. There is no one particular field of work that attracts serial killers as a whole, although as we mentioned earlier, psychopaths are often drawn to powerful, high-status positions within the business world and jobs that require a level head in the face of pressure.

But even so, not every serial killer is a fully-fledged psychopath that craves constant domination in every aspect of their life. What about the disorganized sociopaths and the deluded psychotics? These people have to work somewhere too. The reality is that it comes down to the individual, although in some cases, serial killers may be attracted to jobs that aid their murderous ventures.

Over the years, researchers have uncovered that different types of serial killers can sometimes be attracted to certain types of professions.

Do serial killers tend to work blue- or white-collar jobs?

While it's by no means a concrete rule, one similarity that researchers have unearthed is that organized psychopaths tend to be drawn to professional white-collar roles while disorganized offenders tend to work manual labor positions.

Additionally, it's also important to factor in economical and societal conditions when looking at the jobs of serial killers throughout history. For example, the job market was considerably different during the 1970s and 1980s (the golden age of serial killing), with many manual labor positions of the time now being obsolete. For example, Jeffrey Dahmer worked as a mixer at the Milwaukee Ambrosia Chocolate Factory, a job that is now fully automated today. Therefore, such disorganized offenders may be drawn to different types of work, particularly if they use their professions to find suitable victims.

The killers that would have once been manual labor workers might now turn to tech-based professions to aid their killing in the modern day, but in the end, there are no concrete guidelines that denote a serial killer's profession. It all depends on the individual and socioeconomic circumstances.

What are the 12 most common jobs amongst serial killers?

Michael Arntfield, a criminologist and serial killer researcher, identified a core list of 12 professions that are most likely to attract serial killers. Arntfield looked through the employment history of hundreds of incarcerated offenders and came up with the top three professions for each skill level. These are:

Skilled occupations:

- ⊕ Aircraft machinist/assembler
- ⊕ Shoemaker/repair person
- ⊕ Automobile upholsterer.

Semi-skilled occupations:

- ⊕ Forestry worker/arborist
- ⊕ Truck driver
- ⊕ Warehouse manager.

Unskilled occupations:

- ⊕ General laborer (such as a mover or landscaper)
- ⊕ Hotel porter
- ⊕ Gas station attendant.

Professional and government occupations:

- ⊕ Police/security official
- ⊕ Military personnel
- ⊕ Religious official.

As you might tell, these positions cover a broad spectrum of job types and industries, and very few of them overlap. However, Arntfield claims that many of these jobs might provide the worker with access to potential or vulnerable victims. Arntfield says: "It's a combination of mobility, power (whether structural or actual), and the fact many jobs also simultaneously satisfy the underlying paraphilias, or sexual preoccupations, that also fuel killers."

Did You Know?

- ⊕ Ted Bundy once worked the phones at Seattle's Suicide Hotline Crisis Center
- ⊕ As well as being a children's entertainer, John Wayne Gacy also managed a KFC restaurant.
- ⊕ Joseph DeAngelo, the Golden State Killer, held three of the jobs listed above (police officer, military personnel, truck driver)
- ⊕ While the top three professions for psychopaths are CEO, lawyer, and media personality, there have been zero western serial killers in these professions.

How do serial killers use their jobs to their advantage?

There have been countless instances of serial killers using their jobs to source victims or hide their tracks, but some serial killers have utilized the full length and breadth of their occupations to maximize their murderous endeavors.

Dennis Rader, aka B.T.K., worked as an alarm technician for ADT Security Services. Part of his job was to install alarms in clients' homes. Rader, obviously familiar with these complex alarm systems, would sometimes target houses with these types of alarms and disable them before entering the home. Additionally, once news of the B.T.K. murders reached the masses, the small town of Wichita, Arkansas, underwent an increased demand for home security. Rader's company then sent him to install alarms around the town to protect people from B.T.K., the residents unaware it was B.T.K. himself who was installing them.

Robert Pickton, suspected of being one of the most prolific serial killers in Canadian history, also utilized his unique occupation to help cover his tracks. Pickton was a third-generation farmer, and as a young adult, inherited his parents' pig farm in British Columbia, Canada. Pickton would lure women to his farmstead, blitz-attack, rape, and strangle them. Once his victims had passed away, he would bleed them, gut them, and feed the remains to his pigs. It was also rumored he would grind up his victims' remains, mix them with pork, and sell them to the public.

When police raided Pickton's farm in 2002, they found the DNA of 33 different women on its grounds. Little is known about Pickton's modus operandi since his case is technically still ongoing (as it may involve still-listed missing women). He was officially charged with 27 counts of murder but confessed to a staggering 49.

What are Angels of Death?

Angels of Death are perhaps the most famous of all occupation-based serial killers. They are medical officials who've been entrusted with the care of other people, only for them to abuse their position for their own vile pleasure.

These medical professionals can take the form of doctors, nurses, surgeons, carers, and even therapists. Not only is this type of killer one of the most disturbing, but Angels of Death actually predate modern serial killers by several hundred years. There have been instances of nurses killing patients and children in their care dating back to the 1600s.

The most prolific serial killer of all time, Harold Shipman, was an Angel of Death who operated undetected for over 20 years. He claimed at least 15 victims, all of whom were patients of his whom he overdosed with morphine, but he was suspected of killing up to 250.

Nazi doctor Josef Mengele carried out horrific experiments on war prisoners during the Second World War. After his crimes became known, Mengele gained the moniker "the Angel of Death"; however, medical-based killers predate Mengele by centuries.

What are Angels of Mercy?

Angels of Mercy are a subcategory of Angels of Death, and while their actions are the same, their motives are different. Angels of Death kill for a vast number of reasons, such as control, sexual fulfillment, and the desire to play God. However, Angels of Mercy kill their patients because they believe they're doing them a favor by ending their suffering.

The most famous Angel of Mercy killer of all time, Charles Cullen, killed at least 29 of his patients over a 25-year period and also confessed to murdering up to forty patients. Cullen moved between hospitals around New Jersey, and everywhere that he went, death followed. Cullen would target elderly patients and poison their IV bags with a mixture of lethal concoctions.

When arrested, Cullen claimed that his reason for doing so was to avoid patients getting "coded," which is a medical term for when patients go into cardiac arrest. Cullen believed that if patients went into cardiac arrest, it would dehumanize them.

Why are so many potential serial killers drawn to the medical profession?

As we discussed earlier, psychopaths and the medical industry go hand in hand. The surgeon is the fifth-most popular job amongst known psychopaths, and while the doctor didn't quite crack the top 15, there are undoubtedly many psychopaths working in the field all over the world.

There are numerous reasons why a psychopath - or a budding serial killer - might be drawn to this world, especially those that crave power and domination over their victims. The doctor/patient dynamic is already dominant/submissive, with the doctor assuming the role of the caregiver by default. This immediately addresses a serial killer's desire for authority.

Next, the doctor is naturally assumed to be a figure of incredible moral standing. Even though we might not know anything about the doctor sitting across from us, we instinctively figure that this person has our best interests at heart. This dynamic would also appeal to a serial killer's desire for deceit and underhandedness.

There's also the fact that many of the Angel of Death victims are old and frail. Therefore, authorities might not give much attention to their deaths. This is the main reason so many Angels of Death go undetected for years, often decades. In fact, most Angels of Death are only caught once they've dispatched a considerable number of victims.

Medical workers also have easy access to drugs that could easily take a person's life. Almost all Angels of Death use chemicals from the stashes of their respective hospitals or medical facilities to poison their victims. Doing so also makes it more difficult for investigators to trace the culprit should any foul play be suspected.

What serial killer worked as a grave digger?

Peter Sutcliffe, aka the Yorkshire Ripper, had perhaps the perfect job for a serial killer, working as a grave digger before he began his killing spree.

It was during this job that Sutcliffe claimed he first heard voices from God telling him to kill sex workers. He said that when he sat at the grave of a Polish man named Bronislaw Zapolski, the voices would infiltrate his thoughts and command him to kill.

Sutcliffe was eventually fired from his job as a grave digger because not only was he constantly late for his shifts, but he was also found to be stealing trophies from the dead bodies. He also seemed to have a disturbing sense of humor, often joking about necrophilia with his coworkers. After leaving his stint as a grave digger, Sutcliffe became a truck driver (another ideal profession for budding serial killers).

Did any serial killers pose as employers to lure victims in?

There have been countless instances of bosses murdering their employees and vice versa, but no serial killer, at least in the western world, has used their employee roster as a potential victim pool.

However, the closest instance concerns an unnamed serial killer currently under arrest in Mexico. The man is believed to have posted fake job opportunities on Facebook to lure in young women, and once he had them in a private space, he would blitz-attack, rape, and kill them.

In April 2022, a woman named Viridiana Moreno Vásquez met up with a man in a public café under the pretense of being hired for a job. The role, according to the advertisement she replied to, was a receptionist position that paid $90 per week. CCTV footage caught the two leaving, then Vásquez was never seen again.

According to the arresting authorities, this as yet unnamed serial killer has been pulling this trick since 2013 and may have killed upward of ten women.

What profession is considered the "perfect" serial killer job?

According to an FBI press release in 2016, "If there is such a thing as an ideal profession for a serial killer, it may well be as a long-haul truck driver."

The FBI state there are somewhere around 750 corpses lying along America's roads. Around 2004, it came to light that there was an epidemic of women going missing or being assaulted or murdered at highway truck stops or service stations around the country. So, in 2009, the Bureau created the Highway Serial Killings Initiative in an attempt to boost coordination between various agencies and uncover the reasons behind the exorbitant body count.

Why is truck driving so ideal for serial killers?

Professions on the road often attract the less stable, the transient, and those not so rooted in family life. To them, the road is a never-ending journey of routes, exit stops, and gas stations. People are anonymous, places are mere numbers, and so they seek advantages in the anonymity of the landscape.

Truck drivers live their life in a temporary state. They're barely in the same town for more than a day, and they travel through remote areas that rarely see any human footfall. They can discard bodies in out-of-the-way locations, and by the time the authorities discover the remains, the perpetrator is long gone, in another town, state, or country entirely. Piecing together evidence from a murder scene is already a difficult task, and if the real perpetrator lives five states away, it makes the job significantly more challenging. It also gives killers opportunities to spread evidence farther afield. Dismembered body parts, bloody clothing, and murder weapons can be dispersed hundreds of miles apart.

Another element that makes the road a killer's paradise is its ties to the world of sex work. It's a classic image, the stressed-out, long-haul driver pulling into a truck stop, only to be propositioned by a sex worker. Temptation can easily get the better of them, and so the driver whiles away his stresses in the company of a talented escort.

It's no secret that serial killers often target sex workers, and this is amplified further when we look at serial killers who utilize highways as part of their modus operandi. Sex workers who frequent the streets live a life of vulnerability, often walking into private surroundings with strangers. To a budding serial killer, this makes for perfect conditions to carry out a murder. It's a tragic fact that police do not prioritize most sex worker deaths. A lot of sex worker deaths are not even known about until a body shows up. Combined with the issue of sex workers being reluctant to discuss anything with law enforcement, they make perfect targets for serial killers, especially those who spend long periods on the road.

How many serial killers have actually been truck drivers?

As of the time of writing, at least 25 former truck drivers are serving time in US prisons for serial homicide. However, the FBI estimate there are ten times more unsolved cases of truck driving serial killers than there are solved ones.

Did You Know?

- ⊕ Edward Surratt, a truck-driving serial killer in Pennsylvania and Ohio, claimed over 24 victims before he was finally caught.
- ⊕ Wayne Adam Ford, a long-haul trucker from California, would pick up female hitchhikers on his route, kill them, and keep their bodies in his vehicle for days.
- ⊕ Timothy Vafeades, a trucker from Minnesota, would kidnap young women on the road and lock them in a purposely built torture room in his truck. He kept one victim for up to six months.

- Bruce Mendenhall, a long-haul trucker, claimed victims from Alabama, Indiana, and Tennessee
- Keith Jesperson was a truck driver who assaulted and killed sex workers all across the US and Canada. He left notes with smiley faces at truck stops near his crime scenes.

Are serial killers drawn to the military?

There have been many serial killers who've had previous military experience, but they all seem to have two things in common: their military careers were short-lived and none of them actually saw combat.

Dennis Rader, aka B.T.K., served in the US military as an Air Force mechanic for four years.

Jeffrey Dahmer was enlisted into the US Army in 1979, at the encouragement of his father, becoming a trained medical specialist. He was dishonorably discharged due to his growing alcohol addiction. At the time of his enrollment, he'd already killed at least one person.

Gary Ridgway, the infamous Green River Killer, did a short stint in the US Navy.

Dean Corll, aka the Candyman, who was responsible for the raping, torture and killing of at least 28 young boys, worked as a radio repairman in the US Army.

David Berkowitz was one of the few military serial killers drafted onto the frontlines. Berkowitz joined the US army in 1971 and served in both the US and South Korea.

Are serial killers ever career criminals?

Many serial killers spend their entire lives in trouble with the law before being caught for murder. A lot of serial offenders begin as thieves, voyeurs, and petty criminals before progressing to homicide. However, almost no serial killers have ever been "career criminals" in the sense that their criminal efforts also provided their livelihood.

But there is one historical serial killer that seemingly made his criminal exploits his entire life. Panzram, one of the most brutal, sadistic, and remorseless criminals to have ever lived, seemingly jumped between criminal acts without a second thought. By the time he was eventually caught and hanged in 1930, Panzram admitted to 21 murders, over 1,000 acts of sodomy, and thousands of burglaries, robberies, and arson attacks.

In 1920, Panzram even burgled the home of former president William Howard Taft, stealing enough money to purchase himself a yacht. Panzram would lure soldiers onto his boat, where he would rape and kill them before throwing their bodies into the ocean.

Panzram claimed lives across different countries and continents, burglarizing and robbing people to sustain himself. When Panzram was caught and finally sentenced to death, he told the authorities: "I look forward to a seat in the electric chair or dance at the end of a rope just like some folks do for their wedding night."

Has "going postal" ever applied to a serial killer?

"Going postal" is the term used to describe workplace violence that usually results in murder. The phrase stems from a series of incidents since 1986 where postal service workers engaged in acts of mass killing, shooting coworkers, managers, and members of the general public.

While no serial killers have ever "gone postal," several serial killers have actually worked for the United States postal service.

David Berkowitz, the gunman in New York who shot and killed six people, spent most of his career in the postal service. It was during this time that he began his reign of terror. Although, unlike people who did go postal, Berkowitz claimed to have loved his time working for the postal office. He later claimed that had he not been imprisoned for murder, he would have spent his entire career at the post office.

Robert Shulman was another postal worker-turned-serial killer, and he was responsible for the bludgeoning deaths and dismemberment of five sex workers on Long Island, New York throughout the early 1990s. Shulman would hire the women under the pretense of using their sexual services but then blitz-attack and bludgeon them to death. He would then discard their bodies in various locations around Hicksville, New York.

Have any serial killers ever been involved with politics?

Many serial killers have been drawn to the world of politics in one way or another, and one could argue that many politicians could be considered serial killers by proxy. After all, war, chaos, and death are at the heart of politics, and it's up to our politicians to oppose or encourage these ideals. There is often a polarizing juxtaposition between serial killing and politics, despite the lines between them often blurring. One is evil and condemned, and the other is socially accepted, but both are rooted at the core of the human psyche.

Ted Bundy was drawn to politics in his college university years and took classes in political affairs at the University of Washington. He later took a small role working for the Republican Party, serving on the Nelson Rockefeller presidential campaign in 1968 and being appointed to the Seattle Crime Prevention Advisory Committee - a fact which later proved greatly ironic.

Another notable name in the world of both politics and serial killing was the "killer clown" John Wayne Gacy. The man responsible for the brutal deaths of 33 people was something of a Renaissance man when it came to careers, with occupational ambitions covering a wide range of industries.

Gacy was an entrepreneur who ran his own successful building contractor company. He once worked as a manager at KFC. He was most famously a children's entertainer, dressing up as a sinister-looking clown and dazzling audiences with his magic rope trick. However, he was also a staunch Democrat and a precinct captain in Chicago throughout the 1970s. There's a famous photo of John Wayne Gacy and Rosalynn Carter (wife of Jimmy Carter) together.

BON APPETIT:
SERIAL KILLING CANNIBALS

Cannibalism is one of the most well-known subcategories of serial killers. There's something about the act of physically consuming another human that naturally repulses us, likely because doing so is completely unfathomable to any rational thinker. However, cannibalism is very much alive and well in the serial killer realm, with countless instances of human consumption having taken place throughout the 19th and 20th centuries.

What exactly is a cannibal?

Cannibalism is the act of consuming human flesh. Although, in the realm of serial killers, it can also extend to other forms of human consumption, such as drinking blood (or in the case of someone we'll learn about later, grinding up bone and using it as flour).

Cannibalism has a long, ancient history, stretching back literally millions of years. Anthropological data shows that Neanderthals and Homosapiens often consumed human flesh for nutritional purposes, but with the advent of hunting and eating animal meat, the practice died down over the ensuing centuries.

Many tribes throughout the world maintained cannibalistic practices from the 15th century up to as recently as the 1960s. Some parts of the world believed that consuming human meat provides magical healing properties, and indeed, certain serial killing cannibals held similar beliefs.

What are the motivations behind cannibalism?

While there is no single reason that a serial killer might take to eating their victims, one theme that continually crops up is that of loneliness.

Many serial killing cannibals are loners. Jeffrey Dahmer, Albert Fish, Ed Gein, and Dennis Nilsen - four of the most famous cannibalistic killers of all time - all suffered from crippling loneliness, spending time alone in their homes, although not by choice. All of these killers craved company in one way or another, be it from sexual partners in the case of Dahmer and Nilsen, or by any kind of friend in Gein.

After being apprehended, several cannibalistic killers spoke of a desire to keep their victims with them at all times. These men desired companionship and so transposed the figurative idea of "keeping them inside" into a literal sense by physically consuming human body parts. To the cannibal, this provides a sense of control over their life. Their victim can never leave them.

There may be other motives at play too as each cannibal will have their own reasons for consuming human flesh. Some may do it for the taboo experience. Some may be curious to taste human meat. Some might do it as a form of postmortem power play or out of sexual compulsion.

What does human flesh actually taste like?

According to those who've tasted it (including several cannibalistic serial killers), human flesh actually tastes like pork. While it falls into the category of red meat and has the texture of beef, many have said it tastes like a saltier, bitterer version of pork.

William Seabrook, an explorer who ate human meat during a trip to South Africa said: "*It was like good, fully developed veal, not young, but not yet beef. It was very definitely like that, and it was not like any other meat I had ever tasted... It was mild, good meat with no other sharply defined or highly characteristic taste such as for instance, goat, high game, and pork have.*"

Armin Meiwes, one of the most famous cannibals in history, said: "*The flesh tastes like pork, a little bit more bitter, stronger. It tastes quite good.*"

Is it illegal to eat another person?

Bizarrely, it's not illegal to consume human meat in 49 of the 50 US states. The only exception is Idaho, which is legally able to sentence non-killing cannibals to up to 14 years in prison.

Despite this strangely relaxed law, there are laws surrounding periphery topics that put the topic of cannibalism into a grey legal area. For example, desecrating human corpses is against the law in every state, so sourcing body parts to consume would land any budding cannibal in a world of legal trouble. It's also illegal to own human body parts in all 50 states.

What made the case of the German Internet cannibal so bizarre?

There's no shortage of bizarre cannibal stories out there, but the case of Armin Meiwes, more famously known as "the German cannibal," might be the strangest one of all.

Armin Meiwes was a lonely man who, as a child, desired a younger brother he could "keep forever" by "consuming him." Between the ages of eight and 12, Meiwes began having strong cannibalism fantasies, amplified by his love for horror movies and watching his mother slaughter pigs on their farm.

In 2002, now a fully grown man, Meiwes placed an ad on a website called the Cannibal Café - a place for cannibal fetishists to come together and share their love and lust for eating human meat. In Meiwes' ad, he wrote that he craved a young, healthy man to kill, slaughter, and eat.

Amazingly, Meiwes received considerable replies to his ad. After sifting through the load, he finally settled on a man named Bernd Brandes, and in March 2001, Brandes made the trip to Meiwes's 24-room farmhouse in Kassel, Germany to willingly become a stranger's human meal.

And that was exactly how things played out. Meiwes killed Brandes, dismembered his body, and consumed his remains over the ensuing months. Meiwes was only caught when he boasted of his achievements on the Cannibal Café and a concerned party notified authorities.

Did You Know?

- ✦ The Armin Meiwes cannibal case is a very rare instance of consensual homicide - where the victim willingly encourages their own death.
- ✦ Meiwes captured the entire ordeal on a nine-hour-long videotape. The tape was played in court, causing one of the jury members to pass out.
- ✦ As well as consuming parts of Brandes, Meiwes also ground up his bones and used them as flour for his morbid recipes.
- ✦ Meiwes initially only received eight years in prison for the crime, but this was later changed to life imprisonment.
- ✦ The Armin Meiwes farmhouse where everything took place is now an abandoned property and has since become a hotspot for dark tourists.

Who's the Japanese cannibal that has since become a minor celebrity in his home country?

Japan is known for being an eccentric place, but the case of Issei Sagawa case is almost too farfetched for even the Land of the Rising Sun.

A short, effeminate man, Sagawa despised himself. He hated his feminine appearance: dainty hands, girly voice, petite 4'7" frame. Over time, this self-hatred evolved into an obsession with beauty, particularly feminine beauty, which he saw as a kind of energy that he wanted for himself but couldn't obtain. When he began attending Wako University in Tokyo in 1973, Sagawa already possessed several disturbing inclinations, including bestial and cannibalistic desires alongside his beauty obsession. And it was here that Sagawa took his first real steps toward becoming the deviant he later became infamous as.

Sagawa moved to Paris where he became obsessed with a Dutch woman named Renée Hartevelt.

Sagawa got her alone one night, shot her in the head, and then cannibalized her remains, even spending the night with her partially mutilated corpse. This premeditated attack landed Sagawa in a mental facility back in Japan, but a series of errors awarded Sagawa freedom in record time. Ever since Sagawa has lived as a free man.

But the real bizarre part of the case occurred after Sagawa's release. Strangely, Sagawa became something of a macabre celebrity in Japan, using his crime to propel him to cult icon status. He wrote books about the incident, interviewed on mainstream talk shows, and even starred in some adult films. He also became a guest on TV cooking shows, kind of ironic given Sagawa's cannibalistic actions.

What cannibal has the highest victim count?

While Jeffrey Dahmer is generally considered to be the only cannibal in the western world to have amassed a substantial victim count of 17, one Russian serial killer trumps all when it comes to mass cannibalism.

Andrei Chikatilo, also known as the Butcher of Rostov, was found guilty of 52 murders, many involving acts of cannibalism.

Chikatilo grew up in war-torn Russia in the 1930s and 1940s, and as a child, his mother would often tell him that his older brother was abducted and cannibalized by their starving neighbors. This incident planted a seed in Chikatilo's mind that would echo during his murderous adult years.

Chikatilo targeted a wide range of victim types, including children of both genders and middle-aged women. He would lure them into secluded areas with promises of drugs or alcohol, then restrain and stab them. He then carried out an array of tortures, from gouging out eyes, disemboweling, castrating, and cutting off tongues and noses, many of which he'd then consume. He often imagined that his victims were war prisoners and that he was a hero for dispatching them.

During his court appearances, Chikatilo had to be locked in an iron cage to keep him safe from his victims' family members. He exhibited bizarre behavior during his whole trial, exposing himself, bursting out in violent tirades, and claiming he was pregnant. During the court's final argument, Chikatilo began to sing. He was sentenced to death via a bullet shot to the head, and before he was killed, his last words were: "Don't blow my brains out. The Japanese want to buy them."

Upon his arrest, what historical cannibal was found to have 29 needles inserted into his pelvic region?

Albert Fish was more than just a serial killing cannibal. He was a highly deranged, sadomasochistic sexual deviant who committed some of the vilest atrocities known to man - even by today's standards.

As a child, Fish was exposed to physical abuse at the hands of his parents and caregivers, and rather than oppose it, he actually began to savor the pain. When he was a teenager, Fish took his first foray into sexual deviancy, engaging in hideous acts such as drinking urine, eating feces, and inflicting pain on other young boys.

In adulthood, Fish began to crave pain and torture as he'd received as a child, so he began experimenting with self-harm. He would beat himself with nail-studded paddles and insert cotton balls into his anus, which he'd then set on fire. At the same time, Fish developed a penchant for cannibalism, often eating raw animal meat to quench his desires.

In 1928, Fish abducted a young girl named Grace Budd whom he took to an isolated house, and then killed and dismembered. The girl's disappearance remained a mystery for six years until Grace's family received an anonymous letter detailing how their daughter had died.

Police traced the letter to Fish, and he was promptly arrested. In custody, Fish confessed to a string of vile acts, eventually being found guilty of three child murders (despite claiming he'd killed over 100). A prison examination found that Fish had inserted needles into his pelvis, which he couldn't withdraw. He was sentenced to death by electrocution.

What Baltimore serial killer turned his victims into homemade burgers?

Joe Metheny was a mountain of a man; 6'1 and 450 lbs. He cut an imposing figure with his huge gut and shaved head, and after his wife walked out on him in 1994, he dedicated his life to finding her - and killing her.

Metheny never found his wayward ex-wife, so instead, he targeted the next best thing - surrogates for the woman he hated. Metheny found himself underneath a bridge one night; the same location his ex-wife would buy drugs, and there he found two homeless men he believed knew her. When the men denied all knowledge, Metheny bludgeoned them to death with an axe and threw their bodies in a river.

Metheny served a year in prison for this attack but was then released due to a lack of evidence. He immediately went back to his murderous ways, killing two sex workers. But this time, Metheny brought the bodies home. Deciding to get creative with body disposal, he ground up the bodies and mixed them with beef and pork into burger patties. Metheny then sold these patties to the public through a barbecue stand outstand his house.

When Metheny ran out of "special meat," he'd search for another sex worker. However, one potential victim escaped his clutches and gave the police his information. Upon his arrest, Metheny proudly told the investigators about his human burger business.

Which serial killer abducted women and fed their body parts to each other?

Gary Heidnik was a serial killing cannibal from Philadelphia, Pennsylvania who would capture women and keep them imprisoned in his basement. Here, he would rape and torture them individually, and in one case, he forced his captives to eat one of the others.

To many people, he was Bishop Heidnik, head of the United Church of the Ministers of God. Each Sunday, followers would assemble in Heidnik's home to discuss theology, unaware that there were living and dead women in his basement a few feet below.

Heidnik would target sex workers, lure them to his home under the guise of using their services, and then restrain and dump them into his "pit." He would hold anywhere between three to four women at once and even convinced one of them to become his accomplice. He would punish any captives that didn't behave, either by duct taping their mouths shut or by inserting screwdrivers into their ears.

When one of his captives died, he dragged her body upstairs, dismembered, and cooked it. He then mixed the body parts with dog food and forced his other prisoners to eat it.

Heidnik was caught when his accomplice escaped and informed the police. When authorities investigated Heidnik's house of horrors, they struggled to comprehend the sheer brutality on display. He was sentenced to death, becoming the last person to ever be executed in Pennsylvania.

Did You Know?

- ⊕ Gary Heidnik was one of the real-life serial killers that inspired Buffalo Bill in the 1991 film *The Silence of the Lambs*.
- ⊕ Heidnik's primary motivation was to create a harem of sex slaves.
- ⊕ At least one member of Heidnik's religious group assisted him in the torture of his prisoners.

+ Heidnik inserted screwdrivers into his victims' ears to deafen them so they wouldn't hear him approaching the basement.

+ Before progressing to murder, Heidnik fathered two children with two different women. Both women said that Heidnik would lock them in captivity for long periods.

Who was the Crossbow Cannibal?

Stephen Griffiths was an odd man. Based in Bradford, England, he was a serial killer obsessive who claimed that Ian Brady and Peter Sutcliffe were his idols. He had two pet lizards who he regularly walked on leashes. Some of Griffiths' date partners reported that when they went back to his apartment, he had covered all of the floors and furniture in plastic sheets. As a schoolboy, Griffiths claimed he wanted to be a serial killer when he grew up.

And between 2009 and 2010, Griffiths killed three women with a crossbow and ate their remains.

Griffiths had all the makings of a serial killer from day one. In his teenage years, he was diagnosed as a "schizoid psychopath," and received jail time for slashing the face of a shop owner. His friends claimed that he would feed live animals to his lizards for fun, and one even claimed they once saw Griffiths himself eat a live rat. In 2007, Griffiths started a MySpace page under the alias of "Ven Pariah" and dedicated his page to his love of serial killers.

By 2009, vicarious idolization no longer satisfied him, and so he lured a sex worker back to his apartment. Griffiths then blitz attacked her with a crossbow, killing her instantly. He did the same to two more sex workers, killing them with a crossbow and then dismembering their remains. He cooked some of their body parts and consumed them, while others he ate raw.

CCTV from his apartment complex caught Griffiths in the act of one murder. He was promptly arrested, and when asked his name by authorities, he replied "the Crossbow Cannibal." Psychologists later described Griffiths as a fame-hungry narcissist, who killed women as a passport to infamy.

Who was the cannibalistic "Raincoat Killer"?

Yoo Young-chul was South Korea's deadliest serial killer, claiming 20 lives in less than a single year. In some cases, he even ate his victims' livers.

Very little is known about Young-chul's early life. Everything up until the point he began committing murder - September 2003 - is shrouded in mystery. He began breaking into the homes of senior citizens in his native region of Gochang County, South Korea and bludgeoning them with hammers. He then turned to sex workers, finding them in massage parlors throughout his hometown. He would take them back to his apartment, blitz-attack, and kill them. Then he used scissors to cut them into pieces, ate some of their livers to "cleanse his spirit," then dumped the remains near Bongwon Temple.

Young-chul picked up speed, killing on average two women per month. Interestingly, it was not the police who apprehended Young-chul, but the staff of one of the massage parlors where Young-chul found his victims. He foolishly used one of his victims' phones to call said massage parlor, and the owner recognized the number belonging to the now-missing girl. She informed the police, and they intercepted him.

Because Young-chul was discovered wearing a bright yellow raincoat, the media quickly dubbed him the "Raincoat Killer." Young-chul's motive was that he despised women and the rich, and he was inspired by fellow South Korean serial killer Jeong Du-yeong. Yoo explained his motives in front of a TV camera saying, "Women shouldn't be sluts, and the rich should know what they've done."

Are cannibals legally insane?

No. Serial killers, be they cannibalistic or not, are rarely considered legally insane. While cannibals are likely mentally ill, it would be misleading to label them as insane.

Most cannibals are well aware of their actions, and many go to great lengths to cover their tracks. Furthermore, as we saw in the cases of Joe Metheny and Armin Meiwes, cannibals might even eat their victims as a forensic countermeasure. Authorities can't find victims' remains if no remains actually exist. Many cannibals are highly organized offenders who can understand the difference between right and wrong.

What Asian cannibal killer ate the ashes of his grandfather?

Tsutomu Miyazaki (who we also mentioned in the "Motivations" section), may be the only cannibal in history to technically consume an entire human being in one sitting. Before beginning his murder spree, the Japanese cannibal actually ate the ashes of his grandfather.

Miyazaki, who shared a great bond with his grandfather when he was alive, committed the act to keep his grandfather close to him in death. Psychologists, who later diagnosed Miyazaki, believed that the act may have been what tipped Miyazaki over the edge of madness since consuming human ashes can adversely affect the brain.

Human ashes contain toxins from carcinogenic formaldehyde; the fluid used to preserve the body before cremation. This formaldehyde has been known to cause psychosis in those that consume it.

Which cannibal confessed to over 100 murders, including killing a celebrity's son?

Alongside his partner Henry Lee Lucas, serial killing drifter Ottis Toole claimed to have taken over 100 lives between 1976 and 1984.

Toole and Lucas first met in 1976 at a soup kitchen in Jacksonville, and the two began a homosexual relationship. Together, they drifted between Michigan, Florida, and Texas, creating chaos wherever they lay their heads. Both Lucas and Toole suffered from myriad mental illnesses, with Toole suffering from antisocial personality disorders and pyromania. By the time Toole met Lucas, Lucas had already committed murder - that of his mother.

Across his vast reign of terror, Toole and Lucas carried out at least six murders, with Toole allegedly cannibalizing the remains of some of his victims. When the murderous duo was apprehended in 1983, Texas Rangers reported that the two confessed to an unrealistic 1,000 murders.

Given that both Toole and Lucas were illiterate and mentally deficient, the police knew that Toole and Lucas were confessing to murders they didn't commit. However, the Texas Rangers used Lucas and Toole's willing confessions to close several active unsolved cases, much to the dismay of many.

The team also confessed to the murder of six-year-old Adam Walsh, son of John Walsh, host of *America's Most Wanted*. Toole claimed they picked him up in a Sears mall parking lot, took him to a rural area, and decapitated him. While many cast doubt on the authenticity of Toole's claims, the murder of Adam Walsh was officially attributed to Ottis Toole in 2008.

Did You Know?

- The other major suspect in Adam Walsh's murder was notorious serial killer Jeffrey Dahmer
- Lucas and Toole claimed to have murdered at the request of a cult called "the Hands of Death"
- Ottis Toole married a woman in 1976 but maintained his homosexual relationship with Henry Lee Lucas
- For Lucas and Toole to have committed the murders they claimed to have, they would have had to have traveled 370 miles every day for an entire month
- Toole claimed he committed his first murder at age 14.

What former cannibal now makes a living selling his own unique artwork?

Nicolas Claux, or "'The Vampire of Paris,'" is a French murderer, cannibal, necrophile, grave robber, and self-confessed Satan worshipper. Described by psychologists as a pure psychotic sadist, Claux was convicted of murdering a man in 1994 and subsequently imprisoned in 1997, only to be released in 2002. Today, Claux remains a free man and is something of a celebrity amongst more morbid circles, including occult obsessives and dark memorabilia collectors, of which Claux is an aficionado of both.

Claux's sadistic tendencies led him to apply for jobs in the funerary industry. In 1993, Claux was hired as a morgue attendant at Saint Joseph Hospital in Paris, a position that gave him ample opportunity to indulge his corpse fetish. His duties involved stitching, washing, and prepping bodies for their funeral rites, and when left alone with these carcasses, Claux once again took his ghastly perversions to the next level. It was here that Claux became a fully-fledged cannibal. When alone with the bodies, Claux would cut off segments of flesh, take them home, and consume them.

In October 1994, Claux organized a meet-up with a man he met through a gay chat room. Once together, Claux shot the man in the back of the head with a 22-caliber pistol. Claux was quickly uncovered by authorities, and when they investigated Claux's apartment, they found occult relics, written depictions of dismemberment, a large collection of exploitation films, and most alarmingly, bags of blood in his fridge. The case had all the hallmarks of a fictional serial killer, only Claux was very much real. Due to legal issues, Claux only served five years in prison and has lived as a free man since 2002.

Today, the "Vampire of Paris" is a professional artist, speaker, and niche media personality. While this may sound respectable on the surface, all of Claux's activities revolve around the world of true crime, horror, and occultism. Claux now sells his paintings on his website, all of which depict murder, dismemberment, cannibalism, or the faces of infamous serial killers.

CHASING SHADOWS: UNCAPTURED SERIAL KILLERS

When we hear the term serial killer, we think of familiar names and faces from history who've been plastered over screens and book covers for decades. But the terrifying reality is that the likes of Bundy and Dahmer make up a very small drop in the serial killer ocean. These are the serial killers who've been caught, made mistakes, or were pitted against competent law enforcement and forensic officers that ultimately bested them. Meanwhile, there are hundreds more who evade capture for years, decades, and in many cases, never see justice for their deplorable actions.

Are there any serial killers active right now?

Yes. It's a statistical probability that there are numerous active serial killers haunting the United States - and certainly the rest of the world - at this very moment. The FBI believes that at any one time, there are around 25–50 active serial killers at any given time.

Whether the police or the public become aware of these serial killers is a different story. Quite often, many murders are not publicized, so details are often kept close to those investigating these crimes. However, there have been several (still-ongoing) serial cases in the past decade or so, suggesting that certain serial killers have committed murder and evaded capture, and may still be on the hunt for their next victim.

Perhaps the most famous possibly active offender is the Long Island Serial Killer, an unknown perpetrator responsible for the deaths of at least ten victims between 1996 and 2010. The killer, who dumped his victims' torsos along a wooded area along Gilgo Beach, Long Island, has been the subject of much speculation since his activities were uncovered in 2010.

Are there more uncaptured serial killers than captured ones?

It's very difficult to determine exactly how many uncaptured serial killers are currently in operation. While there are certainly more unsolved murders than solved ones, things work a little differently in serial cases due to serial killer victim counts greatly fluctuating.

Since 1970, there have been around 670 known serial cases in the United States. Meanwhile, there are around 220,000 unsolved murders in the same period. While a fraction of these can undoubtedly be attributed to serial offenders, it's almost impossible to put a solid figure on them due to a lack of information and intelligence. However, the FBI estimate that there are around 25–50 active serial killers at any given time.

What killer mimicked Jack the Ripper in London during the 1960s?

Eighty years after Jack the Ripper terrorized the streets of London, a new, much saucier version of Jack emerged. Like the original monster, Jack the Stripper, named for his tendency to strip his victims' naked postmortem, targeted young working girls near the Bayswater area of London, England. He eventually took at least six lives, one more than the original Ripper.

Also known as the Hammersmith Nude Murders, the naked bodies of six sex workers were discovered around the River Thames between 1964 and 1965. And the similarities between the two serial killers stretch further than their modus operandi, their monikers, and their city of origin. Despite a vast number of suspects and one of the largest manhunts in British history, both of these unknown persons were never caught.

What butcher terrorized the homeless community of Ohio in the 1930s?

Sometimes known as The Torso Murderer, the Mad Butcher was an elusive serial killer who operated in Cleveland, Ohio in the 1930s. He was responsible for the deaths of at least 12 people, all of them being mutilated, decapitated, and discarded in increasingly barbaric ways.

Unlike most other serial killers, it seemed that the Mad Butcher didn't kill for sexual gratification. From what little is known about this mysterious entity, he simply killed because he had an unquenchable appetite for violence. He exclusively targeted the homeless community, disfiguring and decapitating his way through vagrants of any age or gender. Victim characteristics weren't important to him; he was simply a violent brute who killed for the sake of killing.

Authorities believed the Mad Butcher might have been a doctor or surgeon since his decapitations and mutilations were surgically accurate. He was also a strong, large man who could haul corpses for long distances since many were discovered in wooded areas with no vehicle access.

Interestingly, the Mad Butcher's activities may not have begun and ended in Cleveland. Some researchers believed that the Butcher might have moved to another state entirely once he'd slaughtered his way through Ohio and settled elsewhere. In fact, after the Cleveland killings stopped, police received a letter claiming to be from the Butcher:

"You can rest easy now as I have [gone] out to sunny California for the winter. I felt bad operating on those people, but science must advance. I shall soon astound the medical profession - a man with only a D.C. What did their lives mean in comparison to hundreds of sick and disease twisted bodies? Just laboratory guinea pigs found on any public street. No one missed them when I failed. My last case was successful. I know now the feeling of Pasteur Thoreau and other pioneers. Right now, I have a volunteer who will absolutely prove my theory. They call me mad and a butcher but 'truth will out.'"

What modern serial killer might be currently operating in New York?

Known by many names - the Long Island Serial Killer, Gilgo Beach Killer, and Craigslist Ripper - an unknown perpetrator is believed to have killed up to 16 people over 20 years and discarded their remains in ditches throughout the remote town of Gilgo Beach in Long Island, New York.

As recently as 2011, bodies that authorities believe are the handiwork of the Long Island Serial Killer have been unearthed. In total, ten bodies have been discovered, all of which are believed to have been committed by a lone perpetrator. The case regularly goes through resurgences as new leads come and go, and as of the time of writing (September 2022), there is renewed interest in the Long Island Serial Killer case as a new police commissioner has been outspoken about his desire to close the case once and for all.

Did You Know?

- Suffolk County police claimed to have spoken to the Long Island Serial Killer by phone in 2011
- The initial discovery of the first LISK victim was made when police were looking for a completely different victim
- One working theory is that the LISK may be a member of law enforcement, and disturbingly, may actually be a part of the ongoing investigation
- In 2020, Suffolk County police revealed the first piece of evidence in the case - a leather belt with the initials HM or WH inscribed

- The Long Island Serial Killer taunted his victims' families by phone and even used his victims' phones to make the calls.

What uncaptured killer sent victims to watery graves in the Mississippi River?

What are the common murder tools of the serial killer? Knives, guns, ropes, their bare hands. It's very rare for a murderer to utilize an uncommon method of killing, perhaps out of convenience or ease of access. Unless, of course, such a unique killing method is crucial to the killer's personal ritual. While stabbing, shooting and strangulation are by far the most usual methods, occasionally a serial killer will utilize an exceptional tool or strategy to dispose of their victims. Such is the case in the mysterious La Crosse drownings.

Beginning in 1997, multiple people have been found dead in a particular area of the Mississippi River in La Crosse, Wisconsin. Certain authorities believe these are simply freak accidents or statistical certainties, perhaps brought on by inebriation or tomfoolery gone wrong. However, some agencies believe that something more sinister might be at play.

What unique serial killer literally "dispensed" death?

When we think of serial killers, we might imagine cloaked figures ambushing women in alleyways. We might think of home invaders mutilating innocent people in their beds. The term might conjure up images of gun-wielding psychopaths or gloved intruders ready to bring death with their bare hands.

And all of these imagined serial killers have one thing in common: they have to actually be present to commit murder. But what if a homicidal maniac was able to murder from miles away? What if they could lay a trap for someone, so by the time an unfortunate soul happened across it, the perpetrator would be long gone?

Such was the case in Japan in 1985. A mysterious perpetrator laced bottles of soda with a deadly chemical, taking 12 lives across eight prefectures over seven months. More bizarrely, all of these sodas were purchased from vending machines around the country. In perhaps one of the most unique serial killing methods of all time, this unknown assailant literally dispensed death to his victims.

What unsolved case still haunts Finland?

Lake Bodom is a large body of water near the city of Espoo, around 20 miles from Helsinki. A beautiful, scenic part of the Finnish countryside, but one that has since been tainted with the essence of tragedy.

On June 5, 1960, a group of teenagers went camping on the shores of the now-infamous lake. In the early hours of the morning, three of these teenagers were murdered while they slept in their tents in a shocking display of violence, rage, and bloodlust. Some very bizarre happenings took place in the ensuing years afterwards, but the person responsible for the seemingly random massacre has never been caught.

To this day, the homicides that took place at Lake Bodom remain Finland's greatest mystery.

The case was widely discussed across Scandinavia and has become one of the most researched cold cases in the country's history. While the rest of the world may be unfamiliar with the incidents that occurred on that summer morning, the murders left a deep mark on Finnish culture.

The reason for the case's infamy lies in the questions that seemingly lead nowhere. The first mystery is that the weapon used to kill the group cannot be determined and was never found.

In the early years of the investigation, some researchers believed that a scythe was used to kill the teenagers, prompting paranormal-minded researchers to suggest that perhaps the Grim Reaper himself was responsible.

This outlandish belief was also backed up by the sole survivor's witness testimony, who claimed he saw the killer "bright red, dressed in black," moments before he attacked the group.

No trace of the murderer was left behind, and despite confessions from multiple suspects, the true culprit has still never been determined.

What is the "Soka Forest of Horrors"?

In 2014, some locals ventured deep into a forest in Ibadan, Nigeria, and there they discovered a shocking, nightmarish horror scene as if something was ripped from an extreme exploitation movie.

Inside a colonized area of rundown buildings, these locals found rotting corpses, bone piles, human skulls, and even live people chained to slaughter benches. Endless personal possessions of the deceased lay at their feet - passports, clothes, jewelry, and children's toys, suggesting that the true horrors went far beyond what they could see on the surface.

The locals escaped and informed the police, and that was when the rumors began to stir. Was this the site of a death cult engaging in ritual sacrifice? Was this the lair of a lone serial killer, taking advantage of the forest's solitude? Could it be some kind of human farm where body parts and internal organs were removed and sold to the highest bidder?

Police made little headway into the case, despite the massive mound of bodies and evidence to go on. When word of the torture chamber's existence reached the general public, locals were shocked, outraged, and demanded answers from authorities as to how such atrocities could occur without the police becoming aware. But words were not enough, and soon enraged citizens made their petitions to the police through the use of machetes, guns, and blunt instruments.

Exactly what happened inside this forest of horrors - or its reason for existing -remains a mystery to this day. Researchers are convinced that it's somehow linked to cannibalism, ritual murder, or occult practices, but the whole truth is yet to be uncovered.

Who's the most famous uncaptured "highway killer" of all time?

He would come to be known as Washington D.C.'s first serial killer. In the 1970s, a mysterious perpetrator abducted, raped, and killed six young girls throughout America's capital. In five of the cases, he took his victims' shoes as trophies. In one case, the killer left a letter in a victim's pocket, taunting the police to catch him and assigning himself his now-infamous moniker - the Freeway Phantom.

The Freeway Phantom was an unidentified serial killer alleged to have murdered six people between 1971 and 1972 throughout Washington, D.C. The victims were teenage girls, between ten and 18 years old, who were abducted from the streets, most of them displaying evidence of sexual assault upon the discovery of their bodies.

Interestingly, the Freeway Phantom would always collect his victims' shoes, but none of them was ever discovered. One of the victims, Brenda Crockett, managed to call her home after being taken and frantically screamed that "a white man had picked her up". She then hung up but called again a few minutes later.

This time, the man was in the room, and when Crockett's mother's boyfriend asked to speak to him, the phone line went dead. She was found dead the next morning. Despite a substantial effort from the investigators involved in catching the Phantom, they never managed to make an arrest. The killer even taunted them by leaving a note with one of the victims that mentioned that if he ever got caught, he'd confess to everything he'd done.

Among the suspects were the Green Vega group, a Washington D.C. gang responsible for several rape and abductions around the city. One associate of the Green Vega group gave information to the police incriminating some of his fellow gang members, but after the police released the news to the media, he retracted his statement and nothing else came of it. Despite six victims, multiple leads, and several eyewitness accounts who claimed to have seen this mysterious figure, the Freeway Phantom stayed true to his name - a phantom.

Who was the Colonial Parkway killer?

Between 1986 and 1989, the Colonial Parkway thoroughfare in Virginia doubled as a serial killer's hunting ground and disposal site.

Each of the Colonial Parkway killer's murders imitated the crimes of the Zodiac Killer from the prior decade, targeting couples parked in lovers' lanes throughout the Parkway. This unidentified assailant would target an isolated vehicle, shoot the occupants dead and then strangely, drive their vehicles away from the scene and abandon them in a remote location.

The Colonial Parkway killer amassed a total victim count of six, with another two missing and presumed dead. According to authorities, over 130 suspects have been questioned in the 30 years since the murders occurred. However, the case remains unsolved to this day.

Who was the creepy "Maniac with Dull Eyes"?

Sometimes known as the Danilovsky Maniac or the Dull-Eyed Maniac, this mysterious individual was responsible for the murders of at least seven women between 2004 and 2007 in Vologda Oblast, Russia. He strangled his victims with amateur garrotes and skillfully covered his tracks, effectively evading capture despite his high body count. The killer's sadistic activities put the local area in a constant state of fear, to the point that local authorities offered a significant reward for anyone who could help catch the Maniac.

What made the Dull-Eyed Maniac a memorable serial killer was his unique calling card. On the walls of each of his crime scenes, the Maniac left behind crude pornographic drawings.

In addition to this bizarre signature, the Maniac also disposed of every victim inside abandoned buildings or construction sites around the city of Cherepovets. All of the Maniac's victims were women between the ages of 17–31 and they'd all been raped before their slaughter.

Perhaps more creepily than his signature is that, according to reports, the Maniac abducted all of his victims off busy streets in broad daylight, highlighting just how reckless, competent, and skilled this killer was at plying his grisly trade. Between abduction and disposal, the Maniac took his victims to a private space, raped them, and then strangled them to death. And like something out of a Hollywood horror story, the police eventually uncovered this anonymous brute's lair inside an abandoned building somewhere in the city.

But after extensive investigation and 1,200 interviewed suspects, the Maniac was never caught. The case remains cold to this day.

What mysterious killer tormented the Japanese food industry?

Throughout 1984 and 1985, a mysterious perpetrator or group calling themselves The Monster With 21 Faces conducted an extortion and blackmail campaign against several Japanese foods and drinks companies.

Glico, a food company that produced a wide range of Japanese favorites, notably their Pocky and Pretz products, was the main target of the Monster's torment. In March 1984, two men in ski masks abducted the president of Glico, a man named Katsuhisa Ezaki, from his home and took him to an empty warehouse in Ibaraki, Osaka.

The abductors left the man there, but luckily Ezaki was able to escape of his own accord after three days of confinement. After his escape, the Monster With 21 Faces began tormenting Glico and the police with letters, eventually demanding the equivalent of 11 million dollars in payment.

Later, the Monster tormented Morinaga, another confectionary company, with similar letters. Police investigated these threats, eventually recalling numerous products off the shelves throughout Tokyo and western Japan. They discovered over a dozen lethal packages of Morinaga's Angel Pie and Choco Balls, all contaminated with deadly chemicals.

The Monster's operation lasted until August 1985 when they publicly resigned from their reign of terror with a final letter. The police superintendent of the Shiga Prefecture, the man responsible for catching the Monster, committed suicide the same month. The fact he couldn't catch the Monster drove him into a deep depression, so he burned himself alive. The Monster's final letter said:

"Don't let bad guys like us get away with it. There are many more fools who want to copy us. No-career Yamamoto [the police

superintendent] died like a man. So, we decided to give our condolence. We decided to forget about torturing food-making companies. If anyone blackmails any of the food-making companies, it's not us but someone copying us. We are bad guys. That means we've got more to do other than bullying companies. It's fun to lead a bad man's life."

What historical Angel of Death evaded capture for decades after his crimes became known?

Josef Mengele, the original Angel of Death, was a Nazi doctor who experimented on literally thousands of war prisoners to achieve genetic mastery. He was Adolf Hitler's secret weapon in creating an Aryan race, as Mengele was obsessed with uncovering the biological factors that spawned twins.

Mengele was the head of the "selection process," at the Auschwitz concentration camp. When trains of prisoners came in, Mengele would choose who lived and who was sent to the gas chamber. He kept every single set of twins he came across without question. He took great care of them, in stark contrast to how he treated all other children during his selection process. His twins were weighed, measured, and compared to each other in every way. Blood was constantly taken from them, and they were questioned extensively about their family histories. While twins were initially spared from the gas chamber, they were arguably subjected to a crueler fate.

Mengele subjected his patients to extreme, almost-unbelievable bouts of torture. He would castrate them, inject them with chemicals, feed them seawater, submerge them in freezing baths, inject dye into their eyes, and did countless other despicable acts. After the Second World War ended in 1945, Mengele fled from Auschwitz and was never seen again.

Mengele spent the rest of his life evading capture. Neo-Nazi groups protected him in South America, and he was unknowingly assisted by the lack of co-operation by the German government to locate him. In May 1985, German police raided the home of a man named Hans Sedlmeier who was a friend and confidante of Mengele's. The police had been tipped off regarding Mengele and Sedlmeier's acquaintance. Letters between Mengele and Sedlmeier were discovered at the home, and very soon the police were able to track the houses where Mengele had lived in Brazil.

After a thorough investigation, the police discovered that Mengele had reportedly died in a drowning accident in 1979. His death was kept quiet to protect those who had sheltered Mengele after his escape from Germany. The police then discovered the grave where Mengele had been buried, which possessed the name Wolfgang Gerhard - Mengele's fake name since 1971. The body in the grave was exhumed, and forensic tests confirmed that the skeleton buried inside did indeed belong to Dr. Joseph Mengele.

DARK CORNERS:
OBSCURE SERIAL KILLERS

Some of the most fascinating serial cases are the ones that somehow bypass mainstream popularity. For every Jack the Ripper, there are hundreds of similar cases that never achieve worldwide interest, usually due to myriad factors. If a case doesn't have that alluring, somewhat-romanticized appeal, it will often end up an obscure footnote in the annals of true crime. But of course, the obscure cases that sidestep the collective imagination are no less tragic than the ones we're all familiar with.

What lesser–known serial killer was active at the same time and location as Jeffrey Dahmer?

Known as the North Milwaukee Strangler, Walter Ellis sexually assaulted and murdered seven African American women between 1986 and 2007 in Milwaukee, Wisconsin. Ellis's spree began in October 1986 when he strangled a woman named Deborah Harris and dumped her body in a lake. The very next day, Ellis struck again, claiming his second victim whom he strangled and discarded in a back alley.

Strangely, Ellis then went nine years without killing again - a rare occurrence in the serial killer realm. But between April and August 1994, Ellis killed three more women and discarded their bodies in abandoned buildings around the city. Ellis then disappeared for a staggering 13 years before striking again, this time strangling a woman and disposing of her in an empty house.

DNA evidence soon linked Ellis to these crimes. Interestingly, it was discovered that Ellis had also been incarcerated on several different occasions for other crimes between 1981 and 1989 - which explained his long absence from murdering victims during the same years.

Ellis pleaded not guilty at his trial, but the evidence against him was indisputable. He was sentenced to seven life terms. Most interesting of all, Walter Ellis was active at the same time and in the same city as Jeffrey Dahmer. Wisconsin is one of three states to have had multiple active serial killers at the same time (California and New York being the others).

What Michigan killer murdered three of his wives?

Little is known about the crimes of Lowell Amos, but what's known is that between 1979 and 1994, Amos killed four women, all of whom were close to him in some way.

Amos was suspected of killing his mother and his three wives to obtain insurance and inheritance money. Amos was convicted of one count of first-degree murder for killing his third wife, by injecting her with a lethal dosage of cocaine and subsequently sentenced to life without parole. Amos served 18 years in prison for the crime, dying on January 5, 2022 (coincidentally, the same date as his 79th birthday).

Why is the "Monster of the Andes" such a unique serial killer?

Pedro Lopez, also known as the Monster of the Andes, is something of a unique criminal. We know his name. We know what he looks like. We know he's a fully-fledged serial killer. However, we don't know where he is.

Lopez was born in 1948 into a life of misery. His mother, a sex worker, regularly abused him and threw him out of their house when he was just eight years old. He became a petty thief and small-time criminal to sustain himself, ending up in jail at age 18. It was behind bars that Lopez committed his first murder, killing an inmate who raped him.

When he was released back onto the streets of Bogotá, Colombia, he found he could no longer contain his rage. He migrated to Peru and began killing young girls between nine and 12. He then traveled through South America, killing girls wherever he laid his head. Lopez was finally caught in 1979 after allegedly killing "three girls a week for years." It turns out Lopez wasn't lying, as he led authorities to a mass grave in Ecuador containing the remains of 53 young girls.

Lopez was sent to prison, with authorities believing he could have killed up to 300 people. However, Ecuador has a prison term limit of 20 years, so in 1999, Lopez was released into the world. Since then, no one has seen him.

What serial killer hunted humans for sport?

Robert Hansen was a serial killer from Alaska who abducted women and purposely set them free in order to hunt them down.

Hansen was a skilled marksman, an avid hunter, and a former member of the Army Reserve. Moderately wealthy, Hansen purchased a Piper Super Cub bush plane in 1982, then later used it as part of his murderous games. Between 1973 and 1982, he abducted and raped at least 30 women, however, he let them go once he'd finished. But after he purchased his own personal method of air travel, Hansen upped his sinister endeavors considerably.

Throughout the next year, Hansen would target sex workers, abduct them, and take them to an isolated meat shack via his plane. He would then rape and torture them, then release them into the surrounding Alaskan wilderness. Hansen would then stalk them with his .223 hunting rifle, treating his victims like human sport.

After killing them, Hansen would take their jewelry as trophies and then bury their bodies in the woods. He'd mark the burial sites on a map. When police finally apprehended Hansen, this map provided crucial in locating his 17 victims. He was found guilty of 17 murders and sentenced to life in prison.

Who is Finland's only official serial killer?

Michael Penttilä holds a rare honor in the true crime world. He's the only person in the history of Finland who fits the FBI's description of a serial killer.

Penttilä's life of crime began in 1981 when he was just 16 years old. He kidnapped a local teenage girl and held her captive in his basement, where he assaulted and tortured her. Fortunately, the girl eventually escaped Penttilä's imprisonment. Penttilä then chose a target much closer to home: his own mother. In August 1985, Penttilä strangled her in their shared apartment in Oulu, Finland.

A year later, Penttilä coerced two 12-year-old girls back to his apartment under the pretense of giving them alcohol. He locked one girl in his bathroom while he strangled the other. Like his first victim, the other girl managed to escape Penttilä's wrath.

Penttilä was arrested for the murders, but given Finland's lax justice system, he was released only seven years later. A year into his release, Penttilä killed again, this time an older woman whom he choked to death after invading her apartment.

Penttilä was arrested again. Inside prison, he married another murderer, then was released again in 2008. But Penttilä hadn't still learned his lesson. He assaulted several people in the ensuing years, eventually committing homicide again in 2018 when he strangled a sex worker to death. Today, he's back in prison for the third time and remains one of Finland's most notorious criminals. He has considered himself a lesbian since at least 2009.

Who was the Japanese "Hanging Pro" that forced his victims to commit suicide?

Takahiro Shiraishi, aka "Japan Twitter Killer," is a Japanese serial killer who raped, murdered, and dismembered nine people between August and October 2017. He contacted most of his victims on Twitter, targeting people who had suicidal tendencies, claiming that he would like to commit suicide alongside them. However, this was just a ruse.

Shiraishi lured his victims to his apartment where he raped and strangled them to death. Then, he dismembered the bodies of the victims in his bathroom. The body parts would either be put into the freezer or covered by cat litter. Some of the body parts were discarded in the rubbish bin.

Shiraishi took nine victims in total: eight female and one male. The only male victim was the boyfriend of Shiraishi's first victim. The boyfriend contacted Shiraishi and asked him if he knew where his missing girlfriend was. Takahiro Shiraishi then lured him to the apartment and murdered him.

After the last victim went missing, her brother accessed her Twitter account and alerted police to a suspicious handle, leading them to Shiraishi's residence in October 2017, as the killer was spotted with the victim on a surveillance camera at a local train station.

The police then arrived at the apartment and asked where the missing woman was. Shiraishi then confessed all. Police discovered nine dead bodies in the house, all of which had been dismembered. Police found severed heads, legs, and arms placed in freezer boxes and storage containers.

Neighbors corroborated the events by confirming that foul smells of rotting flesh had come from the house. In October 2020, Shiraishi pled guilty to nine murders, and in December 2020, he was sentenced to death.

Who is "the Pusher" of Manchester, England?

The pusher is a very mysterious serial killer, given he may not actually exist. Since 2006, there have been an alarming number of deaths by drowning in a particular body of water in Manchester, England. The drowning site, situated at the heart of Manchester's Gay Village, has been the watery grave of more than 80 men - a disproportionate number of drowning victims in comparison to other bodies of water in similar-sized cities.

Some researchers believe that an opportunistic serial killer is pushing intoxicated men into the canal in the hopes they'll be too disoriented to pull themselves out. The Gay Village is indeed a nightlife hub, and bizarrely, all of the alleged "victims" have been young males. Despite this, Manchester Police insist that the Pusher does not exist, and these deaths are all accidental drownings.

The only opposing piece of evidence to this belief comes from an anonymous man named Tom who claims to have been a victim of the Pusher. Tom said that as he was cycling along the canals one evening, a hooded figure pushed him off his bike into the water. This mysterious perpetrator then kicked Tom's hands away as he tried to claw out of the water. Tom survived the attack, but the mystery of the Pusher lives on.

Who was the Canadian serial killer known as the "Boozing Barber"?

Gilbert Paul Jordan, aka the Boozing Barber, had one of the more unique modus operandi in serial killing history. Jordan would seduce women in bars, take them back to his barbershop, and then pour alcohol down their throats until they died.

Jordan's killing spree began in 1965 and lasted until 1988, although he'd been indicted on several criminal charges before this, including rape, abduction, drunk driving, and car theft.

Jordan would meet women or hire sex workers then get them intoxicated. Once they passed out, Jordan continued to ply them with alcohol until it killed them.

For many years, the connections between the deaths went unnoticed as police believed the women simply died as a result of alcohol poisoning.

It wasn't until an eyewitness linked Jordan to one of the deaths that he became a suspect. Jordan was only ever found guilty of the murder of one woman, but he killed between eight and ten by his own admission and attempted to kill close to 200 women in total.

What Indiana serial killer murdered his own mother as a child?

Charlie Brandt began his serial killing career at a very early age. In 1971 in Indiana, Brandt shot his pregnant mother to death for no apparent reason. He then attacked his father in the same manner and attempted to shoot his sister too, although both survived. Brandt was only 13 years old at the time.

Brandt was then placed in a juvenile center for several years, baffling psychologists as to why this teenager would try and annihilate his entire family. Brandt moved to Florida around 1978 and then resumed his murderous ways the following decade. His next victim, in 1989, was a middle-aged homeless woman who he killed and attempted to decapitate. He also extracted her heart.

By 2004, Brandt had married and moved to Orlando where he lived with his wife and 37-year-old niece. The same year, a hurricane was due to hit the area, so many people evacuated. Brandt chose to stay at home with his wife and niece, and after the hurricane had hit, a neighbor went to check on their wellbeing. Inside, she discovered a horrific scene. Brandt's wife had been stabbed to death in the living room. His niece suffered a similar fate in the bedroom; her heart, head, and internal organs had been diced up. Brandt himself was discovered hanging from the garage rafters.

Investigators found a huge stash of taboo pornography that reportedly belonged to Brandt, some of which involved depictions of women being raped, tortured, and dissected. Brandt was also investigated for his involvement in around 25 murders, although most of them couldn't confidently be attributed to him.

Who was the cruel and sadistic "Toy Box Killer"?

Few serial killers can match the depravity and unimaginable cruelty displayed by New Mexico monster David Parker Ray.

While the true extent of David Parker Ray's crimes may never be uncovered, what we do know is already some of the most disturbing information ever made public record. For more than 40 years, Ray abducted, tortured, and murdered somewhere close to 60 victims, all of whom were subject to excruciating torment through the use of whips, hacksaws, surgical equipment, clamps, blunt instruments, knives, sex toys, syringes, and all manner of homemade equipment.

David Parker Ray's dedication to inflicting suffering motivated him to build a makeshift torture chamber far away from civilization. The "Toy Box", as Ray referred to it, was a soundproof trailer located in Elephant Butte, New Mexico, purposely built to house Ray's captives. While inside, victims would be strapped to a surgical table and forced to watch their own torture through a ceiling-mounted mirror. While Ray's true victim count is unknown, it is estimated to be between 50 and 60, despite him only being convicted of three.

Did You Know?

- Ray would play an audio tape to his victims upon their capture, informing them of the torture they'd be put through. The tape ran for 11 minutes.
- Inside Ray's "Toy Box," investigators found a copy of the book American Psycho, which chronicles the murderous life of a New York investment banker.
- The estimated cost of Ray's torture chamber was around $100,000.
- Ray was only caught when one of his victims, after two days of torture, managed to escape.
- Ray was sentenced to 224 years in prison but died of a heart attack before he served a single day.

Who was the torturous killer "the Candyman"?

One of the more overlooked serial killers of the modern age, Dean Corll is considered by many to be the "original John Wayne Gacy". In the same way that Gacy abducted, raped, and tortured young boys, Corll carried out his crimes in a very similar manner.

In what later became known as the Houston Mass Murders, Dean Corll, along with two accomplices, raped and murdered at least 28 young boys between the years 1970 and 1973. Corll was the mastermind behind the operation, while his two associates, Elmer Wayne Henley and David Brooks, were the ones responsible for procuring Corll's victims and thusly delivering them to him.

Once under his control, Corll restrained his victims onto a homemade "torture board," which rendered them unable to fight back. Then, Corll would subject them to humiliating acts of torture and cruelty - which sometimes last several days. Finally, Corll would sexually assault his victims and then kill them by gunshot or strangulation. On several occasions, he forced his victims to write letters to their parents telling them they had run away from home.

Throughout the Houston Heights area, Dean Corll became known as the "Candy Man" due to his affiliation with the confectionery industry. For a while, he was known as the man who regularly gave out free candy to his friends and locals. Corll was eventually killed by one of his accomplices, who then informed the police of the horrors they'd been involved in.

What Nazi-inspired serial killer murdered people with nail bombs?

David John Copeland was a young, delusional supremacist who would come to be known as the London Nail Bomber. From a young age, David Copeland had an obsession with acts of sadism and cruelty. By the time he was 12, David was reported to have harbored fantasies of being reincarnated as a Nazi officer who would have access to explosives, medical equipment for experimentation, and women to act as his slaves.

On April 17, 1999, Copeland left a nail bomb he'd created using firework explosives outside a supermarket in Electric Avenue, Brixton. At around 5 p.m. that evening, the bomb detonated, causing injury to around 50 people.

A week later, Copeland would plant a second explosive on Hanbury Street. The area is largely known for its Asian culture, which was Copeland's primary target. The bomb detonated on the afternoon of April 24, injuring 13 people.

Copeland's final bomb was left inside a pub in Old Compton Street, a hub for London's gay community. It exploded on the evening of April 30. The compacted area in which the bomb detonated caused horrific, life-altering injuries to a total of 79 people, and caused the deaths of three people, one of whom was four months pregnant.

Copeland was soon identified and inside Copeland's flat, police discovered Nazi flags adorning the walls and newspaper clippings of stories about bomb attacks, in addition to explosive materials, a crossbow, hunting knives, and pistols.

When questioned about his motives, Copeland claimed that he intended to start a race war. He thought bombing minorities would make them lash out, which would be "the spark that would set fire to the country." Copeland was sentenced to six life sentences.

What historical serial killer was believed to have been a practicing vampire?

Béla Kiss was a Hungarian serial killer that preyed on single lonely women, seducing them with displays of affection and promises of marriage. Once these women had fallen for Kiss's charms, he would kill them and preserve their bodies in barrels around his residence. In total, Kiss was responsible for the deaths of 23 women and one man.

Kiss began his crimes around 1900. Kiss targeted women who had no close family and no living relatives, finding them through newspaper advertisements in which he advertised his services as a fortune teller. Women came back to Kiss's home then were never seen again. He had several metal barrels around his home that he claimed were to stockpile gasoline, but Kiss actually used them to aid his murderous ventures.

When World War I broke out, Kiss was drafted into the Austro-Hungarian army in 1914. In 1916, invading soldiers scoured Kiss's home, hearing rumors of Kiss's gasoline stockpiling. Inside the barrels, soldiers were horrified to discover pickled dead bodies. Bizarrely, some of these bodies had bite marks on their necks, suggesting Kiss was something of a practicing vampire.

Authorities in the army were notified, and at the time of the discovery, Kiss was recovering from an injury in hospital. Strangely, there was no sign of Kiss at the hospital, who'd instead placed a dead man on his bed and fled. The war effort aided Kiss's escape, and no one ever truly discovered what happened to the mysterious Béla Kiss.

Did You Know?

- Kiss was possibly sighted in 1920 as part of the French Foreign Legion. But when authorities checked it out, the man in question had vanished.
- In the 1930s, another sighting of Kiss emerged, this time a janitor in New York. Once again, when police checked on him, the man disappeared.
- At his home, police found an alarming number of books on the subject of strangulation and poison.
- Police also discovered Kiss had corresponded with 74 women through newspapers, many of whom were never tracked down.

ONE SHOT: BIZARRE NON-SERIAL MURDERS

In the grand scheme, serial killings only make up a fraction of murders throughout the world. For every multi-homicide at the hands of a single perpetrator, there are over a thousand incidents of singular homicide. Additionally, some of these "one-off" murders may have been the beginning of a serial killing spree if not for the intervention of authorities. Despite them not being serial cases, many of these one-offs are bizarrely fascinating.

What jealous ex-boyfriend killed his former lover and ate her organs?

In September 2014, Tammy Jo Blanton's ex-boyfriend Joseph Oberhansley broke into her home, assaulted, and stabbed her to death. Then, using a jigsaw, he removed part of her skull. After that Joseph carved out a cannibal feast from her body. He cooked and ate part of her brain, heart, and lung.

Police found Tammy Jo's body in the bathtub of her home, covered in a tarp. There were bone fragments found in the kitchen as well as remains. Police brought Joseph in for questioning, a process he was all too familiar with. In fact, he'd had a long history of violent crimes.

When the murder of Tammy Jo was being committed, Oberhansley had been on parole for shooting another girlfriend to death in 1998. He'd also shot both his mother and sister in a previous altercation before injuring himself as well.

While speaking with police, Joseph confessed to the killing and cannibalism. Joseph's lawyers put forth the defense that Oberhansley was insane, a defense that he has denied. He claims that the police never found the actual murder weapon, that he couldn't have done it with the small knife they'd found, and that he took offense at being portrayed as mentally unwell.

Joseph Oberhansley delivered all of this in a ten-minute rant during a pretrial hearing. He was sentenced to life in prison in 2020.

Who was the young girl who "rode her bike to nowhere"?

In the small town of Townsend, Massachusetts, 13-year-old Deborah Quimby went out to ride her bike and never returned home. On the afternoon of May 3, 1977, Deborah left a note for her parents saying she was visiting her grandparents five miles away.

When Deborah never returned, police suspected an abduction. But after some investigating, they discovered some very strange things. In Deborah's school locker was a note written to one of her friends. It asked the friend to meet her because she was upset, and the destination Deborah suggested was her grandparents' home.

Then, more than 30 years later in 2002, police received an anonymous letter claiming that Deborah's body and her bicycle had been dumped in the nearby pond. It was a strange revelation since Deborah's case had long since gone cold and hadn't been recently publicized in the news. Regardless, police scoured the lake but found nothing.

Even stranger still, a second letter was sent to the local police exactly one year later, giving them a specific location to search in the lake. This time, they found items of clothing and rusted parts of a bicycle. Another letter arrived in 2010, telling them to search a wooded area instead.

To this day, Deborah Quimby's body has never been found. It's theorized she was meeting someone, and this person later abducted her. However, the truth remains unknown.

Did You Know?

- The small town of Townsend, Massachusetts has been the site of a disproportionately large number of bizarre crimes.
- Between February and October 1972, nine young women in Townsend were stabbed to death inside their homes. This series of homicides remains unsolved.
- In December 1986, a young boy named Daniel LaPlante stalked a local family by living inside their home without them knowing. A year later, LaPlante murdered another family in town.

- LaPlante's murder victims lived next door to a woman who was a victim of the 1972 murders.
- In 1996, Paul Reed conspired to kill his girlfriend, Stephanie Santerre, with his girlfriend's sister, who he was having an affair with.
- Not only did Deborah Quimby, Dan LaPlante, and Paul Reed all live in the same town, but they were neighbors on same street. Furthermore, this street was aptly named Elm Street!

Who was the murderous YouTuber known as "Mr. Anime"?

Trey Sesler was one of the first ever anime reviewers back when YouTube first launched. He became one of the most popular YouTubers at a time when influencers were still in their infancy. Known as Mr. Anime to his fans, Sesler was considered a normal teenager with a quirky interest. However, over time, Sesler's videos started getting a little darker.

Between reviewing anime, Sesler would upload videos of himself using firearms. Eventually, his reviews became less about anime and more about guns, shootings, and violence. He then released a video entitled "Mr. Anime Is Planning Something," where he told his fans he'd be taking some time off from YouTube.

But on March 20, 2012, Sesler lured his mother into the garage at their home and shot her in the chest with a shotgun. Sesler then located his brother, shooting him with a pistol, and then doing the same to his sleeping father. Sesler then wrecked their house from top to bottom and wrote "I don't know why I did this" on the toilet door.

Sesler's next stop was Waller High School. He drove there and waited outside the building for an hour. Then he drove off.

Police located Sesler with ease, and Sesler was quick to confess. However, no motive was forthcoming. His whole demeanor was cold and distant, and he then revealed his true intentions: to shoot up his old school. Fortunately, for whatever reason, Sesler changed his mind at the last moment. His only confession was that "everything became too real."

Sesler was sentenced to life in prison in August 2012 where he remains to this day.

Who was the young girl who strangely predicted her own death?

In the months before her violent murder, 16-year-old Beverly Jarosz did everything she could to prepare for her apparently inevitable demise. She ruminated on the subject of death, even keeping poems about death in her small black book. "Someone will want to publish these when I'm dead," she told her little sister, Carol.

She studied ways of seeing her future before it came to pass, reading books on parapsychology and palm reading. She locked the doors when she got home from school every day. She always shut her curtains tight. She kept a knife close to her bed "just in case."

This sense that Beverly had fallen within the Reaper's grip began in the summer of 1964, around the time she received an anonymous present tucked into the back door of her family's house in Garfield Heights, Ohio. It was a gift-wrapped box from

Higbee's, tied up in a blue ribbon. Someone had written "To Bev" on the box. Inside was a silver bracelet and ring. She had no clue who had sent it. There were a lot of young men in the neighborhood who wanted to date her, after all. It could have been any one of them. But the anonymity of it frightened her.

Only a few months later, Beverly's father discovered her lifeless body lying face-down in a pool of blood on the floor beside her bed. She'd been stabbed over 40 times in the back and strangled with a rope. There were no clues as to who might have killed this innocent girl. The only suspicious element was a message Beverly had written for her father earlier that day. It said: "Stephen Stackowicz called. Will call back later."

Her father didn't know anyone by this name. Police concluded it was most likely the killer calling to check that Beverly was home. Many suspects came and went, but Beverly's killer was never found.

What young girl was kept captive for eight years?

On the streets of Donaustadt, Vienna in March 1998, a 10-year-old schoolgirl Natascha Kampusch left her family home in the early hours of the morning, only to never arrive at her intended destination. When passing through an isolated area, her kidnapper, Wolfgang Přiklopil, along with an accomplice, dragged Kampusch from the streets into the back of his van. Wolfgang Přiklopil was 36 years old at the time. His motivation for kidnapping Natascha Kampusch was his desire to obtain an "untouched virgin" whom he could one day marry.

At Přiklopil's home, Kampusch discovered that he had been preparing for the arrival of a kidnapped victim for a long time. Beneath Přiklopil's garage was a small cellar that Přiklopil had purposely dug out as a prison for his intended captive. The cellar was around five meters squared in size and boasted reinforced steel doors. No windows adorned the room, and it was entirely soundproof. It would be Natascha Kampusch's home for the next eight years.

Inside her cellar, Kampusch was given books, a TV, and a radio. In Přiklopil's own twisted way, he showed great affection for her. He kept her hidden from the world so that only he was allowed to have her, but at the same time would physically degrade her and force her to perform chores around his house.

In August 2006, the now 18-year-old Kampusch made a successful escape from her living nightmare. Přiklopil had allowed her to vacuum his vehicle in his front garden and Kampusch used the opportunity to flee. She ran to a neighbor's house and begged them to call the police. Přiklopil had previously told her that if she was ever to escape, "they wouldn't catch him alive". Staying true to his word, Přiklopil committed suicide in the hours following Kampusch's escape.

Which wrestling megastar killed his own family and then himself?

Chris Benoit, one of the most respected professional wrestlers of all time, sullied his name forever in June 2007 when he killed his wife and son and then hanged himself — all with no clear motive.

Benoit was an elite athlete and a former World Wrestling Entertainment (WWE) champion with everything to live for. When Benoit no showed a WWE event in June 2007, WWE staff sent police to check on him at his home in Fayetteville, Georgia. There, they found the bodies of Benoit's wife and ten-year-old son strangled to death in their respective bedrooms. Down in the home's gym, they found Chris Benoit hanging by his neck from a weight machine.

The double-murder suicide was a bizarre mystery.

After all, the Benoit family was wealthy and reportedly had no marital issues. Interestingly, on the night Benoit killed his family, he was scheduled to win the WWE Championship (something Benoit would have been aware of beforehand). Before he committed the murders, Benoit called a close friend and told him he loved him, something he'd never done before. He also spent 12 hours with the dead bodies before committing suicide.

One of the most prevalent theories was that Benoit's mental state had been distorted from 20 years' worth of concussions. Upon postmortem analysis, Chris Benoit was discovered to have the brain of an 80-year-old dementia patient (despite only being 40 years old). Chris Benoit has since been whitewashed from wrestling history.

What imprisoned murderer killed Jeffrey Dahmer?

Christopher Scarver was a murderer from Milwaukee, Wisconsin who gained infamy not while outside of a cell, but inside.

In 1990, when Scarver was 21 years old, he was hired as a trainee carpenter. Scarver was promised a full-time position after completing his training, but such an opportunity never came. Scarver left the program, then returned at a later date, armed with a pistol, prepared to extort money from his previous employer.

Scarver found his old boss had left the position, and so turned his rage toward the man's replacement: Steve Lohman. Scarver demanded money, but Lohman only gave him 15 dollars. An enraged Scarver then shot Lohman in the head and left him for dead.

Authorities quickly discovered Scarver and arrested him. He was sentenced to life in prison at the Columbia Correctional Institution in Portage, Wisconsin.

On the morning of November 28, 1994, Scarver was assigned to a work detail with two other inmates, Jesse Anderson, serving time for the murder of his wife, and cannibalistic serial killer Jeffrey Dahmer; the detail included him cleaning the prison gymnasium toilet. When corrections officers left the three unsupervised, Scarver beat the two men with a 20-inch (51 cm) dumbbell bar that he had removed from a piece of exercise equipment in the prison weight room. He returned to his cell and informed a prison guard that "God told me to do it. Jesse Anderson and Jeffrey Dahmer are dead."

Scarver suffered no further repercussions. He later claimed that jailers had purposely left him alone with Dahmer because they wanted him dead.

What makes the death of Elisa Lam so strange?

Elisa Lam, sometimes known by her Cantonese name Lam Ho-yi, was a 21-year-old college student from Vancouver. In January

2013, Elisa paid a visit to California, embarking on what she called her "West Coast tour." Elisa arrived in Los Angeles and checked into the somewhat infamous Cecil Hotel on South Main Street.

Elisa was scheduled to check out of the Cecil Hotel on 31 January, but she never reported to the front desk, nor did she call her parents for her daily check-in. The LAPD were alerted of Elisa's disappearance, and they were unable to find any trace of her at the Cecil Hotel. In the previous days, Elisa had actually made some strange posts on her blog, one of which claimed that she had lost her cell phone.

However, the police did come across something incredibly strange during their search for Elisa. They discovered haunting CCTV footage of Elisa in the hotel elevator, which was soon released to the public and was immediately spread over the internet. The grainy video shows Elisa acting strangely, jumping in and out of the elevator, pushing buttons randomly and seemingly trying to hide from any passers-by. She peeks out of the elevator, as if to make sure no one is watching, then finally walks off and out of frame. No one other than Elisa was captured on the video. It was the last known footage of her alive and was time-stamped the same date she disappeared.

On February 19, 2013, a maintenance person for the hotel went up to the roof to inspect the Cecil Hotel's water tanks, and in one of them, he found the naked, dead body of Elisa Lam. Her clothes - the same ones she was wearing in the CCTV footage, were floating next to her. It was a shocking discovery that raised many questions, and theories and speculation began to run wild. The only clear answer that could be gleaned was that Elisa died of drowning and had been inside her watery grave for three weeks.

Everything else, including how she managed to even get inside the tank, was a mystery.

Did You Know?

- ✦ The Cecil Hotel, where Elisa died, has a long and somewhat morbid history. In the past, three famous serial killers have walked its hallways.
- ✦ Some sources claim that to gain access to the hotel roof, Elisa would have needed to break into areas of the Cecil that were off-limits to hotel guests.
- ✦ The circumstances around Elisa's death mimic the plot of the 2005 horror film *Dark Water* to bizarre levels.
- ✦ Eerily, there was a deadly outbreak of tuberculosis just after the discovery of Elisa's body. In an almost unbelievable coincidence, the tuberculosis test kits deployed by hospitals were named LAM-ELISA.
- ✦ Given the elevator footage and the toxicology reports, the majority of evidence pointed toward Elisa suffering a psychotic break and losing control of herself.

What soldier decapitated his wife's lover and gave her his head as a gift?

The case of Stephen Schap is so unbelievable that it's commonly believed to be nothing more than an urban legend. In 1993, Schap, a serviceman in the armed forces, discovered that his wife had been cheating on him with another soldier named Sergeant Glover while Schap had been overseas. Worse yet, his wife was nine months pregnant with the other soldier's child.

Schap returned home, hunted down his wife's lover, and killed him. He then removed his former friend's head with a hunting knife, placed it in a bag, and drove to the hospital where his wife was due to give birth. Upon arrival, he showed his wife the severed head of her lover, still with blood and entrails hanging from the neck. Schap then claimed, "Look, Diane, here's Glover! He can sleep you with every night now. Only you won't sleep because all you'll see is this!"

The case was so bizarre that many considered it untrue until the court transcripts were made public. One section read:

> *"Placing the severed head into an athletic bag, appellant took it to the hospital where his wife had been admitted when it was feared she might be suffering a miscarriage (of a child by the deceased). To the horror of his wife and hospital personnel, appellant burst into her room, pulled the head out of the bag, deposited it on her bedside tray table, and physically forced her to look at it."*

Schap was arrested immediately. He received a life sentence for his actions.

What killer murdered six people in a fitting revenge attack?

Li Yijiang, while certainly an unhinged killer, could be considered something of an antihero. In December 2002, six men raped the 25-year-old Yijiang at a local disco. Yijiang had contacted the men through a gay dating site and agreed to meet them there for explicit fun but not to the extent that took place.

The men poured alcohol into Yijiang's throat and once he was sufficiently intoxicated, the men sexually assaulted him. When

Yijiang returned home, he began plotting his payback. Over the following six months, Yijiang was able to lure the men individually to isolated locations around Beijing, and there, he killed and castrated them.

Police discovered that all the men had talked to the same user through the same dating site, it led them to Yijiang. He was arrested in August 2003, and he happily confessed to murdering the six men and removing their genitals. In his native land of China, he was affectionately known as the "Penis Slasher." Shortly after Yijiang was apprehended, the firing squad executed him.

Which heavy metal musician killed one of his bandmates?

Louis Cachet, professionally known as Varg Vikernes, is a pioneering musician in the black metal genre. This genre, not for the weak at heart, is characterized by heavy music, diminishing chord progressions, satanic imagery, and morbid lyrical themes. While most black metal musicians tend to play characters, certain members of the community take things to the extreme.

Varg Vikernes was one such community member. After getting into an argument with his bandmate Euronymous about royalties, Vikernes headed to Euronymous's apartment in Oslo and stabbed him to death. Vikernes claimed that he carried out the murder because he believed his bandmate was going to kill him first. Allegedly, a mutual friend of them both had informed Vikernes that Euronymous planned to abduct Vikernes, tie him to a tree, and make a snuff video of his murder. These claims have never been confirmed.

Vikernes went to jail for 21 years (the maximum allowed in Norway) then was released. He has since returned to making music.

Did You Know?

- ⊕ Euronymous's intentions have never been confirmed, but Euronymous did have a sadistic side. He once found the dead body of a bandmate who'd committed suicide, and then photographed the corpse and used it as an album cover.
- ⊕ Due to black metal's connection to satanic religions, many black metal devotees took to burning churches in the scene's early years, resulting in several deaths.
- ⊕ The black metal scene has been the backdrop of many brutal murders since the early nineties.

Who killed his own mother over concert tickets?

Robert Lyons was a big Avril Lavigne fan. So much so that when his mother refused to buy him tickets to see her in concert, he killed her.

Lyons, a 39-year-old from Chicago, got into a heated argument with his mother, 61, when she refused to oblige her son's request for gig tickets. Driven by rage, bashed his mother's head in with a cognac bottle then stabbed her nine times in the back then poured chemicals over her body. Lyons then drove around town, visited a bookstore, then called the police and confessed to what he'd done. Police found him in a local Hooters.

Lyons reportedly suffered from myriad mental illnesses and had recently been off his medication. He later claimed it was never his intention to hurt her. Lyons was sentenced to 40 years in prison where he remains to this day.

What serial killer–obsessed girl committed her own murder in 2016?

Jemma Lilley was obsessed with serial killers and violence from a young age. As a child, she would roleplay as a serial killer and collect butcher's knives. At 15, she wrote her fiction novel that documented the exploits of a serial killer named S.O.S. (inspired by real-life serial killer Son of Sam).

In 2016, 25-year-old Lilley struck up a friendship with a girl named Trudi Lenon, and the two forged a relationship based on BDSM dominant and submissive roles. After several months together, Lilley and Lenon mutually decided they would kill together. Their victim was an 18-year-old man named Aaron Pajich who had learning disabilities and went to the same college as Lenon. They invited Pajich to Lilley's house and when his back was turned, stabbed him to death.

Authorities were quick to trace the murder to Lilley and Lenon. In court, the two blamed each other for the crime, but both were sentenced to life in prison. Lilley's stepmother later said that Lilley was a disturbed, odd child from day one and constantly made her feel on edge. So much so that she was unable to share a home with Lilley and moved out the first chance she got.

DEVIOUS DELINQUENTS: KIDS WHO KILL

On average, serial killers commit their first murder at 27 years old. But of course, some killers start much younger. There's been no shortage of murderous children over the years, with some even killing before they reach their teenage years. For the purposes of this section, we've categorized kids who kill as anyone up to the age of 18 as this is the age juveniles become adults in the eyes of the law.

Who is the youngest serial killer ever?

At an age when most children are riding bikes and playing with toys, Amarjeet Sada was committing murder. Sada, from the village of Musahar in Bihar, was only seven years old when he took a life for the first time. A year later, he took two more, making him the youngest serial killer of all time.

Little is known about Sada's murders due to his age, but it's believed that in 2006, Sada murdered his six-year-old cousin with a knife. He later suffocated his baby sister, only eight months old at the time, and then finally killed a six-month-old that lived in the same village.

Although no clear motive was ever put forward, a child psychologist described Sada as a sadist who derived pleasure from killing. Due to him being a minor at the time of his crimes, Sada was released after a stint in juvenile detention and now lives as a free man, although his whereabouts are unknown.

Are juvenile killers tried the same as adults?

In most cases, juvenile killers are bound by different laws than adults. The maximum sentence that juvenile offenders can receive is two years imprisonment providing they're between 16–18 years old. For 12- to 15-year-olds, the maximum time they can serve is one year. Anyone younger is judged based on individual factors. The juvenile system tends to focus on rehabilitation whereas the adult system focuses on punishment.

In very extreme cases, juvenile killers can be tried as adults if their crimes are violent enough to warrant it. This is a very polarizing subject that's been the subject of intense debate for many decades. The decision as to whether a juvenile should be tried as an adult comes down to the judge of the particular juvenile court. Factors they'll consider are:

- The seriousness of the offense and whether the child caused serious harm to another person.
- The age of the juvenile.
- The juvenile's record of criminal activity.
- Whether the juvenile is amenable to treatment. Someone not amenable would be a juvenile who has already

received counseling and other services but continued to commit crimes.

What teen murderer was inspired by a genre of music known as "horrorcore"?

In 2009, 16-year-old Emma Niederbrock met a boy on MySpace. Emma, a self-confessed "outsider" from Farmville, Virginia, used social media to connect with like-minded people. She was a part of the "horrorcore" subculture—a genre of rap-rock music with a focus on morbid lyrics, themes, and imagery.

The boy Emma met was 18-year-old Richard McCroskey, but he went by the online moniker "Syko Sam." McCroskey, an aspiring horrorcore artist from California, was Emma's dream guy. He was mysterious, brooding, and had that tortured genius appeal she found so fascinating. Before long, Emma and McCroskey forged an online relationship.

The two made plans to meet up at a festival and afterwards go back to her parents' place in Virginia. Emma believed it was going to be the start of a romantic, fruitful relationship, but the truth was much different. In the flesh, McCroskey was very shy and timid, a far cry from the sinister character he portrayed online. Not only did she find him unattractive, but she also found him repulsive.

During the festival, Emma ignored McCroskey and did her best to escape him, despite his advances. Once the festival was over, Emma made good on her promise to let McCroskey stay at her place. They slept in separate bedrooms. Emma's mother and her best friend Melanie also stayed in the house.

The next day, Emma, her mother, and Melanie were found bludgeoned to death in their beds. McCroskey, driven by a jealous rage, brutalized them with a sledgehammer and then fled the scene in a stolen car. Police discovered McCroskey the following day asleep in an airport baggage area, awaiting a flight back to California. He was charged with first-degree murder and sentenced to life imprisonment.

What famous poisoner started his killing career as a teenager?

From a young age, Graham Young developed a strange fascination with poisons. While his school friends were dating and playing sports, Young was holed up in his bedroom devouring books on the subject of poisons and famous poisoning incidents. This would only be the beginning of a life of bizarre obsession.

Young's eccentric tendencies began from the moment he was born. As a child, he rarely said a word, choosing instead to play with toys and immerse himself in books. When he began school, he never socialized with any of the other children or spoke to the teachers. He was a lonely child by choice.

At the age of 13, Young walked into a chemist and convinced a pharmacist to sell him incredible amounts of arsenic for "research purposes." Young used his vast knowledge of toxicology to convince the pharmacist that he was much older than he appeared. He used the chemicals to poison a classmate of his, but the classmate survived.

When Young was 14, members of his family showed signs of excessive poisoning regularly. Young soon began to focus his attention solely on his stepmother Molly. In November 1961,

Young's father found Molly lying in the back garden in excruciating pain. She was clenching her stomach and violently throwing up. More sinister, however, was that Young simply watched her suffer as she rolled around the floor in agony. Molly was rushed to hospital the same evening, eventually succumbing to her wounds. It would later become clear that Young had poisoned Molly with thallium.

Authorities traced the incident to Young, who was then admitted to a psychiatrist at the request of his school, where his endless know-how of poisons, famous poisoners, and toxicology became known. At age of 15, Young was considered to be too dangerous to live a normal childhood. He was then admitted to the now-infamous Broadmoor Mental Hospital for a minimum of 15 years, becoming the youngest patient in Broadmoor history.

Did You Know?

- ⊕ A fellow inmate in Broadmoor suffered fatal cyanide poisoning within months of Young being admitted to the mental hospital. He later confessed to the murder.
- ⊕ Young claimed that he continued studying poisons whilst inside the mental hospital, extracting required ingredients from plants in Broadmoor's yard.
- ⊕ At age 24, Young was released from Broadmoor. He began his killing ways immediately, claiming two victims within two weeks of his release.
- ⊕ Young soon found work at a photographic laboratory in Hertfordshire, then later poisoned his boss.

- After being arrested and sent to Parkhurst Prison for his adult murders, Young became good friends with another British monster, the "Moors Murderer" Ian Brady.
- Young died at 42 from heart failure, although some people close to him believe he poisoned himself.

What teen killer stalked a family by living inside the walls of their home?

Daniel LaPlante was a troubled young boy who endured a miserable childhood. At 16 years old, LaPlante became infatuated with a girl in his town named Tina. The two first began talking over the phone, and Daniel told Tina that he was an attractive, blond, athletic boy - a far cry from the truth. When Daniel and Tina eventually met up, Tina was horrified to discover that she'd been flirting with a grungy, greasy-haired, acne-ridden boy who looked nothing like his description.

Daniel and Tina went on a few dates, then Tina broke things off with him. She thought she'd never see Daniel again, but around the same time, Tina and her family began experiencing bizarre events around their house. Things would go missing. TVs mysteriously turned themselves on. Music blared from nowhere. They'd hear knocks against the wall throughout the night. Tina and her sisters believed they were being haunted by the spirit of their recently deceased mother.

After Tina and her family came home one night, they found their entire house in disarray. There was even a message written in shaving foam on the walls - "I'm in your room. Come find me."

Tina's father opened a closet and found a figure - concealing their face with makeup - waiting inside with a hatchet.

The family ran into a bedroom and locked themselves inside. They heard the figure raiding the house, but Tina managed to escape through the bedroom window. She went to their neighbor's house and called the police. When the police arrived, they found a house in disrepair, but no sign of the intruder.

Two days later, Tina called the police again when the knocking returned. This time, a team of police officers scoured the entire house from top to bottom. After almost giving up, one officer broke down a false wall in the basement, and behind it, found a figure living inside the three-by-three-foot space. The boy was Daniel LaPlante. He'd been stalking and watching Tina and her family for over six months.

Daniel went to a juvenile facility for a year, but when he was released in October 1987, he went straight back to his delinquent ways. In December 1987, he broke into the home of a family in town, raped and murdered the pregnant mother then drowned her two young children in the bath. LaPlante was promptly caught and sent to prison where he remains to this day.

What senseless murder shocked Britain in 1993?

Few crimes shock and appall the nation to the extent of the murder of James Patrick Bulger. The body of a two-year-old boy was discovered at a railway line in Liverpool, England, some two miles from where he was last seen several days earlier. His injuries were horrific, demonstrating one of the most serious cases of abuse ever witnessed in a case of this kind. To make matters worse, the perpetrators were revealed to be two ten-year-old children.

Robert Thompson and Jon Venables were children themselves when they repeatedly attacked and ultimately murdered a defenseless toddler. The severity of their crime raised key questions about our understanding of inherent evil, and the level of disturbance that would drive two children to commit such an atrocious series of acts against such a vulnerable victim.

Young Bulger was led away by these two older children from a local shopping center to secluded railway lines. The two older children repeatedly tortured the boy, leaving him with numerous horrific injuries that in their own right could have been fatal. Suffering unimaginable cruelty, Bulger was left to die on the track, intentionally laid there by his attackers. The age of criminal responsibility suggests that legally, neither of the attackers could be deemed to have been criminally responsible for their actions. Both attackers have since been given new names, but their identities are regularly leaked.

What Asian teen poisoned her own mother and documented it on social media?

While her name is unknown, the Shizuoka's Schoolgirl's crimes certainly aren't. This 17-year-old girl from Shizuoka, Japan poisoned her own mother and documented the happenings on her social media blog. The girl, whose name has never been released due to her age, was reportedly obsessed with infamous British poisoner Graham Young.

On August 18, 2005, the girl reportedly dosed her mother's food with thallium - the same poison used by Young. Within a few minutes, the girl's mother became violently sick, and the girl made notes of her mother's ailments in her notepad.

Over the next few weeks, the girl regularly dosed her mother with the thallium she had purchased from the chemist, continuing to document the effects on her blog.

Authorities were informed of the blog's contents, by which point the girl's mother had fallen into a coma and was being monitored in hospital. Police discovered someone in the local hospital matching the descriptions in the blog and investigated immediately.

They traced the blog back to a home in Shizuoka. There, they seized the young girl's computer and found that she was the author of the blog in question. In the girl's bedroom, the police found all manner of strange materials: dismembered dolls, animal heads, bizarre drawings, various drugs, and a stash of thallium.

The girl's mother died in the months following her poisoning. She remained in critical condition until passing away at an unknown date and time. The fate of the girl herself remains unknown due to the confidentiality of the case, however, it is believed that she now resides in a Japanese mental hospital.

What artificial cyber crush resulted in the tragic suicide of a 13–year–old girl?

Due to the growing popularity of social networking sites, anyone can assume the role of a teenager. Such was the disturbing case of

Lori Drew, who posted online as a 16-year-old boy so she could infiltrate her own daughter's social circle - and with tragic results.

Lori's daughter Sarah had been friends with a 13-year-old girl named Megan, but the two had recently fallen out, and Megan was reportedly bad-mouthing Sarah around their school in Michigan. To find out what Megan was saying about Sarah, Lori created a fake MySpace account. Her alter ego was named Josh Evans; a handsome 16-year-old boy who'd just moved to Michigan from Florida. According to his profile, Josh was home-schooled and played guitar and drums in his spare time.

Lori, or "Josh," struck up a friendship with Megan through MySpace. Before long, the two had a romantic attachment, although they'd never met up in real life. Once Megan became attached, Lori extracted the information she needed about her daughter. Then "Josh" turned aggressive. He began insulting Megan, making fun of her appearance and personality. After an hour-long tirade of abuse, Josh broke off his friendship with the distraught Megan.

Megan, who suffered from anxiety and relied on anti-depressants, went to her bedroom and hanged herself with a belt. Unfortunately, Lori Drew was only convicted of three misdemeanor charges for unauthorized computer access.

What murderous teen claimed to be a 500-year-old vampire named Vesago?

Rod Ferrell was a murderer and self-proclaimed cult leader from Murray, Kentucky. Ferrell, born in 1980, murdered at age 16, branding his victims with a "V" mark to signify the murder was the work of his vampire cult.

In 1996, Rod and two accomplices broke into the home of Naomi and Richard Wendorf. While Richard was sleeping, Ferrell bludgeoned him to death with a crowbar, fracturing his ribs and skull. He then found Naomi asleep in another room, but Naomi awoke and threw hot coffee at her attacker. Ferrell got the upper hand and bludgeoned her to death in the same way as he had her husband.

Ferrell and his accomplices then drove through four different states over the next four days. One of Ferrell's accomplices had called her grandmother while they were in Baton Rouge, Louisiana, and the grandmother informed the police of their whereabouts. They were promptly detained in Louisiana and extradited to Florida.

The victims were the parents of a girl named Heather Wendorf, a friend of Ferrell's. Ferrell's motive for the murder was that he was helping his friend escape from her home life. Ferrell was sentenced to death for his role in the murder, making him the youngest ever prisoner on death row. However, this sentence was later changed to life imprisonment.

Who was the only US killer to be executed for a crime he committed under the age of 17?

Sean Sellers, a devout Satanist, killed his own mother and stepfather in 1986 before claiming he was possessed by a demon.

Sellers crept into his parents' bedroom as they slept in their Oklahoma City residence, then shot them both in the head. Sellers then tried to engineer the scene, so it looked like the murders were the result of a robbery gone wrong. At the time of the killings, Sellers was only 16 years old.

At his trial, several defenses were put forward by Sellers' attorneys. They argued that the murders were the work of a deluded Satanist. They claimed he was addicted to *Dungeons & Dragons*. And much to everyone's surprise, Sellers actually confessed to additional murder while in the courtroom. He claimed that he killed a local store clerk who'd refused to serve him a beer in 1985. This was later confirmed.

In a controversial move, Sellers was sentenced to death by lethal injection. Many people opposed the decision, including high-ranking political figures throughout the world. However, in February 1999, Sellers was executed at Oklahoma State Penitentiary. In the days leading up to his execution, he denounced Satanism and converted to Christianity.

What strange catfishing love triangle turned deadly in 2006?

In 2005, a middle-aged, married man named Thomas Montgomery began posing as an 18-year-old marine. According to his dating profiles, he'd just returned from Iraq and was looking for love. He soon struck up an online relationship with "TalHotBlondbig50," an alleged 17-year-old stunner from West Virginia named Jessie.

The two corresponded daily, exchanging saucy pictures (all of which Montgomery stole off the Internet and passed off as himself). Jessie returned the favor, sending bikini and beach snaps across to her online lover. Before long they were texting daily - but had never actually met.

Then Montgomery's wife discovered his extramarital flirting and contacted Jessie herself. She sent Jessie an email showing what her balding, overweight husband really looked like. Jessie was shocked, and as an act of confirmation, she contacted one of Montgomery's colleagues. The colleague, a man named Brian Barrett, verified that Montgomery wasn't who he said he was.

Weirdly, Jessie then struck up a fresh romance with Barrett instead. At their workplace, Barrett would regularly boast of his new 17-year-old love, often within Montgomery's earshot. The frustration mounted. Montgomery had been outed as a cheater and an online pervert, and in September 2006, Montgomery could no longer contain his rage.

He waited at their factory for Barrett to finish his shift. When Barrett clocked off and headed toward his car, Montgomery shot him three times with a .30-caliber rifle, instantly killing him. Police had no problems tracking Montgomery down, and once he'd been arrested, their next stop was to interview Jessie.

In a fitting conclusion, it turned out that "Jessie" was a middle-aged housewife who'd catfished both Montgomery and Barrett with pictures of her 17-year-old daughter.

What 13-year-old convinced her boyfriend to annihilate her entire family?

In 2006, a vengeful 13-year-old girl convinced her boyfriend to murder her mother, father, and brother - all because they disapproved of her relationship.

The girl (whose name has never been made public due to her age), orchestrated one of the most violent and tragic murders in Canadian history. In April 2006, the duo stabbed the girl's parents to death, as well as her younger brother who was just eight years old. The court transcripts detail a disturbing scene: the young brother pleading with his sister to spare his life. The girl stabbed him twice in the chest, and then handed her brother over to her boyfriend who slit the boy's throat.

While it was the boyfriend who delivered the death blows, courts ruled that the girl had purposefully encouraged and persuaded him to kill her family.

This emerged after several witnesses had come forward to testify that they had heard her say that she hated her family and wanted them all dead, while others had overheard her asking her boyfriend to kill them.

Several hours after the brutal killings, the couple was spotted kissing and laughing in a nearby restaurant. The same night, they were overheard boasting of the murders at a party, with the boyfriend telling horrified guests that he had gutted his girlfriend's family "like fish."

Both were arrested the following day. In jail, the two swapped gushing love letters and the boyfriend proposed. His still-smitten girlfriend accepted.

The jury reached its verdict in four hours. Both were guilty, making the girl the youngest person in Canadian history to be convicted of murder. She currently resides in a mental facility but will be released in the ensuing years.

Did You Know

- After the case was closed, further strange findings came to light
- The boyfriend allegedly believed he was a 300-year-old werewolf and often drank his own blood
- Both were members of several gothic-based social media sites, with the boyfriend claiming his purpose in life was "blood, destruction, guts, gore and greed"
- He also wrote poetry, and in one poem he described how he was going to murder his girlfriend's parents by slitting their throats
- The girl posted several pictures of herself online holding handguns.

DEATH IMITATES ART:
KILLERS INSPIRED BY MEDIA

Art imitates life, life imitates art. Every day, people are inspired by the figures they see on screen or read about in books, whether it's absorbing a hero's no-nonsense approach to justice or being inspired by a villain's sinister ponderings. Media can have a great effect on our personal outlook, and indeed, many murders have been the product of misplaced inspiration at the hands of protagonists from books, TV, and films.

Who was the teen killer inspired by Jason Vorhees?

Like many other teenagers in the 1980s, Mark Branch had a particular fascination with horror films. However, the Greenfield, Massachusetts teenager took his obsession to the next level. On October 24, 1988, he killed an 18-year-old college student while dressed as Jason Vorhees from Friday the 13th.

The mutilated body of Shannon Gregory was discovered in her bathtub by her sister. She had lacerations on her chest, abdomen, and head. Immediately, Mark Branch was considered a suspect after police spoke to some of his classmates, however, Branch had coincidentally vanished.

It then came to light that Shannon had been writing a psychological evaluation of Mark Branch for her psychology class; something which Branch wasn't pleased about. A search of Branch's home uncovered 75 horror films, 64 true crime books, three knives, hockey masks, and various weapons.

The search for Branch lasted a month. Soon, Branch's car was discovered abandoned in the Greenfield woods. On November 28, 1988, Branch's body was discovered hanging from a tree in the same area.

Branch's death was ruled a suicide, however, rumors around the town state that the locals dispensed vigilante justice.

What is the "Matrix defense"?

The *Matrix* defense is one of the more creative ways criminals have attempted to skirt the justice system. It's the argument that offenders shouldn't be punished for their crimes because they believed they were living in a simulated reality when they committed, similar to the premise of the hit movie franchise *The Matrix*.

The defense was birthed in 2003 during the case of Joshua Cooke, a 19-year-old who killed his adoptive parents. Cooke was obsessed with the 1999 film *The Matrix*, even copying the style of the film's protagonist Neo. In February 2003, Cooke purchased a 12-gauge shotgun similar to the one used by the film's main character, then later used it to shoot his mother and father. Cooke

144

then called the police, claiming he wanted to test whether or not he was actually living in a virtual reality himself.

The Matrix defense, a subcategory of the insanity plea, was put forward in Cooke's trial. However, Cooke was found to be sane, receiving a 40-year prison sentence for his crimes.

What deluded murderer killed 12 people during a showing of a Batman movie?

In July 2012, audiences all over the world queued up to see the latest installment in Christopher Nolan's Batman franchise: *The Dark Knight Rises*.

In one theater in Aurora, Colorado, a psychotic gunman threw a tear gas grenade into the audience and then opened fire with a rifle. The audience screamed in horror, but the gunman - a 24-year-old named James Holmes - took 12 lives and injured 70 others (62 directly and eight indirectly).

Holmes was arrested on site. Sporting wide eyes and bright orange hair, many people quickly made connections between Holmes's appearance and that of the famous Batman villain 'The Joker'.

During interviews with psychiatrists, Holmes continually referred to the shooting as "the mission." As a child, Holmes was allegedly haunted by what he called "Nail Ghosts," which were imagined manifestations that would fire rifles at each other. Holmes is now in prison for the remainder of his life.

What Stephen King book inspired at least four people to commit murder?

Stephen King has pumped out almost 70 books in his long and storied career, but there's one book of his that's so controversial it's been out of print for decades.

Rage, one of King's books written under the pseudonym Richard Bachman, deals with a harrowing subject even by King's standards. The main character is a dejected school student who takes revenge on his classmates by holding them hostage with a rifle. The story features many casualties of the boy's unbridled rage, and it seemed that many real-world people found inspiration in the main character's actions.

The book inspired a young boy named Jeffrey Lyne Cox to take his fourth-period humanities class hostage in 1988, resulting in the death of one. It also influenced a teenager named Dustin Pierce from Kentucky to take 11 classmates hostage the following year.

There was also Barry Loukaitis, a teenager who killed his teacher and two students and wounded another student during his fifth-period algebra class in 1996. Lastly, in 1997, Michael Carneal unloaded his rifle upon a prayer group in the lobby of a Kentucky high school, murdering three people and wounding a further five.

The controversy around the book prompted King to gradually phase the book out of production. Since 1998, no new copies have been printed. In a 2013 essay entitled "Guns," King discussed these shootings and explained his reasons for discontinuing the book:

"I pulled it because in my judgment it might be hurting people, and that made it the responsible thing to do."

What killer was inspired by *Robocop*?

Nathaniel White was a serial killer who took the lives of six women across New York between 1991 and 1992 while on parole. But most bizarre was his motive for committing these crimes: he claimed he was inspired by the film *Robocop 2*.

White would lure women into his vehicle, take them to a secluded location, and stab them. Police initially suspected White because the sister of one of the victims caught him leaving a club with her one night. Upon investigation, White confessed to the murder, followed by another five. He led police to their dumping grounds: railroad tracks, abandoned buildings, and hillsides around the Hudson Valley region of New York.

Under interrogation, White explained his desire for murder had come as a result of watching the film *Robocop 2*, which sees a futuristic law enforcement officer infiltrate the underground drugs trade. White said:

> *"The first girl I killed was from a* RoboCop *movie...I seen [the character] cut somebody's throat then take the knife and slit down the chest to the stomach and left the body in a certain position. With the first person, I killed, I did exactly what I saw in the movie."*

What potential serial killer was inspired by the hit show *Dexter*?

When Police discovered the crimes of Canadian independent filmmaker Mark Andrew Twitchell, they believed he was on track to becoming a serial killer. Thankfully, police intervened before Twitchell was able to reach the requisite three murders to reach serial status.

Instead, police caught Twitchell after his first murder and, while the crime was shocking in itself, what stood out was Twitchell's strange source of motivation.

Authorities believed that Twitchell had been inspired to kill by the popular TV show *Dexter*, the plot of which sees a forensic worker - a crime scene blood spatter expert - track down serial killers outside of his work commitments. Dexter Morgan is not only a serial killer hunter but a serial killer himself.

Twitchell, himself a filmmaker, even shot a short film about a vigilante murder with the same sequence of events that he later carried out in real life. Twitchell placed an ad on an online dating service posing as a woman to lure in a potential victim. A man named John Brian Altinger responded to Twitchell's ad, and the two met up outside a rented garage, with Altinger believing he was going to have sex with his date partner and then leave.

However, Altinger was never seen or heard from again. Fortunately, he had contacted his friends beforehand and told them where he was headed. Police then investigated and found the garage belonged to Mark Twitchell. Once Twitchell's name reached the news, a second potential victim came forward and claimed that he too had been lured to that garage and attacked by a strange man in a mask.

Who copycatted the crimes of the Zodiac killer?

As well as finding inspiration in books, TV, and films, some killers find inspiration through the most associated sources - other serial killers. One such case concerned that of Eddie Seda, who mimicked the infamous Zodiac killer.

Aside from Jack the Ripper, the Zodiac might be the most notorious uncaptured serial killer of all time. Across five years in the 1960s, the Zodiac killed at least five people in San Francisco, all while taunting the press and police about his murderous endeavors with letters and cryptic puzzles. Despite decades of searching, the Zodiac has never been discovered.

Twenty years later, a Zodiac copycat emerged — the first of its kind. Heriberto "Eddie" Seda began his reign of terror in November 1989, first sending cryptic clues to the press and police suggesting that he might strike in certain locations. Police initially dismissed it as a hoax, but then the bodies began piling up.

Seda took a more literal approach to the "Zodiac" name, only killing people when certain stars were visible in the night sky. The New York Police consulted a professional astronomer, who confirmed that their killer was indeed making good on his promises.

After shooting and killing three people, eyewitnesses led police to Seda, who then confirmed his guilt through fingerprints he left on his notes. Seda engaged in an hour-long shootout with police in 1996, but Seda lost the battle and was arrested and convicted of the Zodiac copycat crimes. After his arrest, psychologists found that Seda was obsessed with astronomy.

What two girls stabbed a girl because they saw visions of the fictional creature Slenderman?

In May 2014, a 12-year-old girl named Payton Leutner was almost stabbed to death by two deluded young girls who believed they were being commanded by a fictional horror character.

Slenderman is a tall, faceless creature who began life as an entry for a Photoshop horror contest. The image took hold of the Internet's collective imagination, with extensive lore and fanfiction having been written about him. Quite often, Slenderman is said to take shelter in forests.

Two 12-year-old girls, Anissa Weier and Morgan Geyser, lured their best friend Payton Leutner into a wooded area in Waukesha, Wisconsin under the guise of playing hide and seek. Suddenly, the two girls attacked Leutner, pinning her down and stabbing her a total of 19 times in the arms, legs, and torso. Weier and Geyser then fled the scene and left Leutner for dead.

However, Leutner managed to crawl to a nearby road where she attracted the attention of a passing cyclist. She was taken to the hospital and revived - luckily, considering she was apparently only minutes away from death by the time she got help.

Weier and Geyser were apprehended the same night around five miles from the crime scene. Police found the bloody knife in Weier's bag. Both girls admitted to the attack, apparently lacking empathy, and claimed the stabbing was required to appease Slenderman's wishes.

Weier was charged with attempted first-degree homicide and Geyser with attempted second-degree homicide. Due to the severity of the crime, both girls were tried as adults. Weier was found to suffer from schizophrenia and was sentenced to 25 years to life in prison. Geyser was awarded the maximum sentence: 40 years to life.

Did You Know?

- ✧ The Slenderman stabbing sparked fierce debate about the effects of Internet stories on children—a debate that will continue for decades
- ✧ The incident has sparked many films, documentaries, and fictionalizations, including an episode of the popular crime series *Criminal Minds*
- ✧ Leutner survived the attack and said she's come to terms with the incident, and she's no longer traumatized by it
- ✧ Leutner also said she would thank the girls for what they did because it encouraged her to pursue a career in medicine.

What killer was inspired by *Halloween* villain Michael Myers?

John Carpenter's *Halloween* (1978) is one of the most iconic horror films of all time, laying the groundwork for the countless slasher films that followed. It introduced the world to Michael Myers, the white-masked psychopath obsessed with tracking down and killing his sister.

While *Halloween's* 1981 sequel wasn't as critically acclaimed as its predecessor, it marked the first time the character of Michael Myers inspired a violent crime in reality. The sequel film saw

Myers invade the residence of an elderly couple to steal a kitchen knife, which he then used to murder the family in question.

In December 1982, a man named Richard Delmer Boyer followed the same sequence of events, reportedly inspired by the popular film. Boyer snuck into the home of Francis and Eileen Harbitz, stole a knife from their kitchen, and stabbed the elderly couple to death. Their bodies weren't discovered until their son William checked on them five days later.

William discovered Francis in a sitting position in the hallway surrounded by blood. His wife was positioned in the kitchen, face down, covered in lacerations. Autopsy results showed a total of 43 stab wounds between them.

When William tried to connect the pieces together, he remembered that Boyer had done yard work for his parents in the past and recalled that Boyer seemed to have a violent demeanor about him. Naturally, suspicion fell on him. A search of Boyer's home in El Monte, California, unearthed a bloody knife that connected him to the crimes.

What famous serial killer was obsessed with *The Exorcist III*?

Jeffrey Dahmer is undoubtedly one of the most heinous serial killers in history, and given his excessive media coverage, we often think we already know everything there is to know about the Milwaukee Cannibal. However, not a lot of people know that Jeffrey Dahmer was reportedly obsessed with a particular horror movie.

Dahmer had a VHS copy of the *Exorcist III* (1990), which he told detectives he watched up to three times per week for six months in a row. The film's plot revolves around a detective's chase for a serial killer known as the Gemini, long considered to be dead. Strangely, one of Dahmer's victims even watched the *Exorcist III* with him, unaware that Dahmer was being inspired by the events on film.

He had lured 32-year-old Tracy Edwards to his apartment, then snapped handcuffs on him when he was intoxicated. Dahmer then pulled out a large knife, put on the *Exorcist III*, and told Edwards he was going to eat his heart. Luckily, Edwards managed to escape the apartment, which then led to Dahmer's arrest.

What murdered was inspired by *The Purge* franchise of films?

Inspired by the polarizing political landscape of modern America, James DeMonaco's *The Purge* (2013) asks the question: *"What if murder was legal for 12 hours?"*

But for 19-year-old Johnathan Cruz of Indianapolis, Indiana, this question was more than just the plot of a fictional movie. He took the question as a challenge. Cruz was a self-proclaimed leader of a local Bloods gang who shot three men in the head in May 2016. Cruz chose all of his victims at random.

Police discovered the first dead body on North College Avenue in the early morning of May 12, dead by two gunshots. They found the second on North Denny Street a few hours later, shot three times. The third victim was found in the driver's seat of a Pontiac on North Linwood Avenue, also shot twice. On the final night of Cruz's four-day reign of terror, a local girl tipped off police about

Cruz's actions and even revealed to them that Cruz was motivated by a film.

The girl told police that Cruz was her drug dealer and explained how Cruz had recently been bragging about shooting three men to death. She also revealed that Cruz had attempted to show her a video of one of the murders. This led to Cruz's arrest.

Incredibly, Cruz's phone was stacked to the brim with evidence confirming his guilt. One of his texts read: *"I Purge every night now. Since I'm dying, someone else has to."* Cruz even sent his mother a screenshot of a news article about one of his murders, asking his mother to "delete this after you read it."

His mother, perhaps more technologically advanced than her teenage son, informed Cruz that police could easily pull up his or her deleted history. Under interrogation, the Purge-inspired shooter confessed to everything and was eventually sentenced to life without parole.

What killer inspired by the horror doll Chucky committed Australia's worst mass killing spree?

Martin Bryant was a mentally ill loner who found solace in horror films. His obsession grew over the years, culminating in a brutal spree that took the lives of 35 people — the worst mass killing spree in Australian history.

In Hobart, Australia, Martin Bryant grew up alone; with no friends, bullied by his classmates, and socially awkward. Bryant would speak ill of his peers and wish them dead. The only pleasure he found in life was horror films and diving trips with his doting father. Bryant had learning disabilities and an IQ of 68 - two things that made his entire life a struggle. Only when he reached prison did doctors diagnose him with Asperger's Syndrome.

But Bryant's troubles were obvious from day one. He tortured animals, set fires, and had a particular, unsettling obsession with animals and humans having sex with each other. Something else he obsessed over was the horror film *Child's Play 2*.

After completing his special education curriculum in 1988, Bryant took a job as a gardener and was introduced to wealthy 59-year-old heiress Helen Harvey. The 21-year-old Bryant quickly shacked up with Harvey and inherited almost half a million dollars when she died in a car accident (that Bryant was also involved in but survived).

In 1993, Bryant's father was found mysteriously drowned with a diving weight belt around his neck, leaving yet another inheritance to Bryant. By this point, Bryant was incredibly wealthy, closing in on millionaire status. But even though Bryant had an easy life, he was still driven to one of the most violent acts Australia had ever seen.

Across two days in April 1996, Bryant committed what came to be known as the Port Arthur Massacre, taking the lives of 35 people in less than 48 hours. It was the worst mass killing by a single person in Australian history. Bryant moved between cafes, gift shops, toll booths, and gas stations, gunning down anyone who happened to stand in his way with a semiautomatic AR-15 rifle. His victims ranged in age from three to 72 years old. By the time he was captured, Bryant had killed 35 and injured 23 people.

After Bryant's actions reached the news, one of his ex-girlfriends came forward to describe Bryant's personality. She said:

> "He loved Chucky and used to go on about it all the time. It comes to life and has to kill this boy so it can be real and then it just goes around killing all these people. There was a phrase in that movie that he used to say, 'Don't fuck with the Chuck.' He used to get excited when he'd say that. He would think he was really cool."

SERIAL KILLERS
IN POP CULTURE

Today, names like Ted Bundy and Jeffrey Dahmer are as well-known as Marilyn Monroe or Mother Teresa. Scroll through TV listings or any streaming service and you're sure to find an overabundance of shows either detailing the life and crimes of famous serial killers or perhaps a fictionalized account of their stories. In today's world, serial killers are intertwined with popular culture, represented as plentifully as celebrity actors or musicians.

What serial killer has been depicted the most in pop culture?

No serial killer has infiltrated popular culture quite like Jack the Ripper. The mysterious phantom who terrorized London in 1888 has since become the worldwide gold standard for evil, whose crimes are now the subject of countless films, TV shows, video games, theater plays, books, and comics across the globe. Despite the Ripper having never been caught and his victim count quite low in comparison to similar crimes, Jack the Ripper appears to be the benchmark to which other serial killers are compared.

Most famously, the Ripper's crimes were depicted in the 2001 film *From Hell* starring Johnny Depp. More recently, the Ripper was featured in several games in the popular *Assassin's Creed* series of video games. In London, near where the Ripper's crimes took place, there is a museum dedicated entirely to the Ripper. The murder sites where the Ripper's crimes took place now foster a macabre tourist industry.

Who was Norman Bates, the original pop culture serial killer icon?

Norman Bates, first created by author Robert Bloch in his book *Psycho* (1959), then adapted into a film a year later, arguably began the modern obsession with serial killers. In the book and film, Bates is the proprietor of the Bates Motel, and while he's a handsome, young, shy boy on the surface, Bates is actually a serial killer with a dissociative identity disorder. He has a deep bond with his deceased mother, whose identity he assumes on a nightly basis.

The character of Norman Bates was believed to have been inspired by grave robbing ghoul Ed Gein, who shares Bates's obsessive bond with his mother, and also assumed her identity by wearing skin suits made of the corpses he stole. However, Bloch took creative liberties with the idea, transposing Gein to a different time and placing him in a more suburban setting.

What real-life serial killer inspired the Hannibal Lecter character?

People often think that Dr. Hannibal Lecter, the main protagonist in *The Silence of the Lambs* franchise, is a purely fictional creation. However, author Thomas Harris has since stated that Lecter was inspired by a real-life murderous surgeon named Alfredo Ballí Treviño.

When Treviño was a medic intern in 1959, he slit his own lover's throat with a scalpel after a particularly violent argument. Treviño then cut the body up into little pieces and buried it in a disused lot.

Thomas Harris met Treviño when he was on assignment in the Monterrey Prison in Mexico. Harris initially believed that Treviño was a prison doctor, but only after talking to him did Harris realize Treviño was an inmate. Harris claimed Treviño was a "small, lithe man with red hair who stood very still and spoke elegantly." He passed away in 2009 at 81 years old.

Interestingly, in a real-life event eerily similar to that of Hannibal Lecter and Clarice Starling, serial killer Ted Bundy was actually consulted by detectives on another serial case. In 1986, detectives from Oregon flew to Florida to meet Ted Bundy in prison, who at the time was awaiting execution.

Bundy had read about the murders of the Green River Killer the same year and offered his insight to help catch him. Bundy told detectives that the culprit was most likely revisiting the sites he dumped bodies, and this was how detectives eventually caught the Green River Killer. It is unknown whether or not Harris used this scene as inspiration for the plot in *The Silence of the Lambs*, but many of the similarities are uncanny.

Did You Know?

Buffalo Bill, the secondary antagonist in *The Silence of the Lambs* was inspired by five different serial killers:

- Ed Gein, because the character skinned women and wore their flesh as clothes.
- Edmund Kemper, because Bill reportedly killed his own mother (book only).
- Gary Heidnik, because he kept his victims imprisoned in his basement.
- Ted Bundy, as Bundy also pretended to be injured to lure women into his van.
- Gary Ridgway, the Green River Killer - who weighed his victims down in bodies of water. At the time of the book's writing, Ridgway was still unidentified.

What real-life killers were inspired by the *Scream* series?

In 1996, the first *Scream* movie hit our screens and, through its subtle lampooning of movie tropes, breathed new life into the horror genre. The film dealt with the subject of a masked killer terrorizing teens throughout the fictional town of Woodsboro, but many people don't know that while the concept was nothing new, the plot was inspired by a famous serial killer named Danny Rolling.

In August 1990, after being kicked out of his parent's home by his father, Rolling set up camp in a wooded area of Gainesville, Florida. He then snuck into the apartments of two college students, stabbing one to death, then raping and stabbing the other. The following day, he did the same to another college student. Two days afterwards, he did the same to another three victims, stabbing one so forcefully that he ruptured her heart.

It took two years for the police to identify Rolling as a suspect, but he finally confessed to all six murders. He claimed that his motive for doing so was to become famous. He was executed by lethal injection in October 2006.

Did You Know?

- Bringing the wheel full circle, the *Scream* series itself has actually inspired several copycat murders over the years
- Two teens, Daniel Gill and Robert Fuller, stabbed their 13-year-old friend after watching the first *Scream* installment
- Mario Padilla, a 16-year-old boy from Lynwood, California, stabbed his own mother in what later became known as the "*Scream* murder"
- Thierry Jaradin, a lonely 24-year-old truck driver, stabbed a 15-year-old girl to death while wearing the movie's iconic Ghostface mask.

What is murderabilia?

Serial killers have become such a pop culture phenomenon that it's even led to a collecting industry boom. Murderabilia is the hobby of collecting items relating to infamous serial killers and criminals, with many high-profile pieces now sitting in museums and personal collections around the world.

Many alternative celebrities, such as rock stars and artists, have dabbled in the industry. Musicians Marilyn Manson and Jonathan Davis (from the band Korn) possess many notable pieces, with Davis even once owning Ted Bundy's famous Volkswagen Beetle. However, the most famous murderabilia collector of all is "outsider artist" Joe Coleman.

Coleman, known for his grand canvases that detail the lives of infamous criminals, owns a vast array of notorious artifacts, including a confession letter from Albert Fish, murder weapons used by Gary Heidnik, some of Charles Manson's hair, and even a personalized painting from John Wayne Gacy. Coleman maintains all these pieces in his New York home, and viewing is possible through invite only.

While the majority of pieces are housed in personal collections around the world, several high-profile pieces can be glimpsed in museums. The aforementioned vehicle of Bundy's is on display at the Alcatraz East Crime Museum in Pigeon Forge, TN, alongside John Wayne Gacy's worn clown suits. The bunkbeds where the famous Heaven's Gate cult committed suicide can be seen in the Museum of Death (alongside many other strange pieces) in Hollywood, LA.

Did You Know?

⊕ The origins of the modern murderabilia industry can be traced back to the 1950s when a carnival owner bought Ed

Gein's car and charged people admission to see it at his show.

- Common murderabilia items include handwritten letters, prison artwork, crime scene relics, hair and nail samples, and personal items of clothing.
- The most expensive piece of murderabilia ever sold was the Colt Cobra Revolver of Jack Ruby, the man who killed Lee Harvey Oswald. It sold for two million dollars in 2008.
- The most expensive piece of murderabilia still available on the market (as of September 2022) is John Wayne Gacy's last ever painting. It's currently available for $49,000.
- One of the rarest pieces of murderabilia of all time, currently in the collection of Joe Coleman, is the business card of William Marwood - a British hangman from the 1800s.

What is the "Son of Sam law"?

The law prevents convicted criminals in many states from profiting from their crimes, either through selling their life stories directly to book publishers, film producers, television networks, or any related industry. The Son of Sam laws are based on the notion that when a person commits a crime, they lose certain rights and privileges, including the ability to sell their story for financial gain.

The Son of Sam laws were introduced as a direct result of the celebrity status attained by New York serial killer David Berkowitz, aka the Son of Sam. In 1977, after hearing reports that Berkowitz was being offered a large sum of money for the rights to his personal story, the New York State Assembly passed a law requiring that a convicted criminal's income from creative works describing their crimes must be deposited in an escrow account.

The funds from the escrow account are then to be used to reimburse crime victims and their families for the distress, harm, and trauma they've been put through.

Has any popular media actually been produced by serial killers or murderers themselves?

A lot of serial killers have written books while incarcerated, be it fiction or non-fiction.

Perhaps the most famous serial killer-written book of all time is the *Gates of Janus*, penned by infamous child murderer Ian Brady. In the book, Brady recounts his life story, as well as provides an "analysis of serial killing." Brady psychoanalyzes several other famous serial killers, including John Wayne Gacy, Peter Sutcliffe, Ted Bundy, and Henry Lee Lucas.

The Gainesville Ripper, Danny Rolling, was another budding wordsmith, penning two novels whilst behind bars. His first book, The Making of a Serial Killer, discusses his abusive childhood and goes into detail about the five murders he committed. After this, Rolling wrote a fiction book called *Sicarius*, the bizarre plot of which involves a zoologist hunting down an alien relic amongst an African tribe.

John Wayne Gacy also wrote his autobiography whilst behind bars, a book called *A Question of Doubt*. In it, Gacy declares his innocence and makes up excuses for how 33 dead bodies could appear underneath his floorboards.

Gerard John Schaefer, a serial killing police officer, also wrote a collection of short stories entitled *Killer Fiction*. Each story, which involves a brutal and senseless murder, bears more than a few passing resemblances to Schaefer's own crimes.

Who was the real-life serial killer that appeared in the Exorcist?

The Exorcist (1973) has something of a reputation. Not only is it considered one of the most terrifying films ever made, but there's also something known as "the *Exorcist* curse." The film has been associated with a series of brutal events, including deaths, fires, and unexplained events. However, the most unnerving piece of trivia is that a real-life serial killer actually played a role in the original *Exorcist* film.

In one scene in the film, a radiographer played by actor Paul Bateson carries out medical tests on the film's main character. Bateson was a real-life radiographer at the time, hired by the director for the realism he brought to the role.

A few years later, Bateson fell on hard times, turning to binge drinking. In September 1977, Bateson broke into the home of a Hollywood reporter and stabbed them to death.

Shortly after his arrest, William Friedkin, the director of *The Exorcist*, visited Bateson in prison.

There, Bateson admitted that he'd committed additional murders, and indeed, Bateson had been a suspect in a series of murders along the Hudson River that saw gay men dismembered and discarded in bags. However, Bateson was never officially connected to these murders.

Bateson was released from prison in 2003 and has never been seen or heard from since. It is unknown where Bateson is or whether he's still alive.

Did You Know?

- Actor Jack MacGowran, who played film director Burke Dennings in the film, died of influenza before the film was released.
- Vasiliki Maliaros, who played Father Damien Karras' mother, also passed away that same year before *The Exorcist* hit the big screen.
- During the production, a number of the cast and crew, including Linda Blair, who played Regan, and Max von Sydow, who played Father Merrin, also lost family members.
- During filming, the set for the main character's home burned down. Eerily, the only part that survived was the bedroom where the exorcism scenes were shot.
- In total, nine real-life deaths took place throughout the nine-month period of the film's shooting.
- The soundtrack of the film also uses actual audio recordings of the real-life exorcism of a 14-year-old boy.

What TV show depicts the life and career of famous FBI profiler John Douglas?

Mindhunter (2017) is a crime thriller TV show based on the illustrious career of famed FBI agent John Douglas. Douglas was instrumental in creating the art of behavioral profiling, a psychological science employed by law enforcement agencies across the world today.

The show looks at the early years of behavioral science and how Douglas was able to adapt it from a small idea into a widely accepted and crucial branch of the FBI.

The show sees Douglas analyze and interact with a vast array of infamous serial killers, including Charles Manson, Edmund Kemper, Jeremy Brudos, Wayne Williams, David Berkowitz, Elmer Wayne Henley, Richard Speck, Tex Watson, and Paul Bateson (mentioned above). While not named the same, the two main characters represent John Douglas and his partner Robert Ressler.

Did You Know?

- ✦ Many of the interviews in the show are re-enacted almost word for word from Douglas's recordings and transcripts.
- ✦ One of the most famous scenes sees Holden Ford (Jonathan Groff) locked in an interrogation room with an irate Edmund Kemper. The scene was inspired by real events.
- ✦ Douglas himself was a consultant on the show, ensuring that the fictionalized events matched the real events as closely as possible.
- ✦ Edmund Kemper, one of the few serial killers referenced in the show still alive at the time of its airing, watched the show in prison and said the actor's depiction of him was excellent.

- Many scenes were filmed in prisons where the real killers themselves had once been incarcerated.

What Stephen King books were inspired by serial killers?

Iconic horror author Stephen King finds inspiration in all of the world's dark corners, so it's only natural that at some point he would fictionalize a famous serial killer or two. King has actually done this three times throughout his vast body of work.

The first came in King's novel *Misery* (1987). The plot sees a deranged nurse capture her favorite author and torture him until he writes a novel that, unlike the author's recent output, satisfies her. King based this deranged nurse on a real-life counterpart named Genene Jones. Jones was a pediatric nurse and Angel of Death who may have killed as many as 60 of her patients.

The next came in 2009 with King's novella *A Good Marriage*. The story's plot involves a typical suburban husband who leads a double life. By night, he's a sexual predator and serial killer, killing local women and taking their jewelry as trophies. The character was inspired by Dennis Rader, aka B.T.K. Weirdly, Rader claims to have read the book while incarcerated.

Another serial killer-based character of King's is James Rennie Junior from *Under the Dome*. Junior, a paranoid psychotic, descended into absolute madness once the ominous glass dome imprisoned his hometown. Junior, who becomes a serial killer and necrophile, was actually based on Ted Bundy. And while unconfirmed, John Wayne Gacy may have inspired the killer clown Pennywise from IT.

On the flip side of the coin, a real-life serial killer carried out a series of attacks between 2010 and 2017 that grimly echoed the plot of a Stephen King story. *The Lawnmower Man* (1975) deals with the subject of a murderous gardener who kills a man who hired him for a landscaping job. Bruce McArthur, a 66-year-old landscaper from Toronto, murdered at least eight men in a series of brutal attacks, scattering their remains in flowerpots around their own gardens.

What film is based on the life of Henry Lee Lucas?

Henry: Portrait of a Serial Killer is one of the most unique serial killer films ever made. It follows the life of Henry Lee Lucas, a real-life drifter and murderer who coasted through the USA killing people at random. He struck up a relationship with a fellow drifter, Ottis Toole, and the two embarked on a nationwide murderous rampage.

The film shies away from typical tropes as there's very little plot. Much like Lucas's real life, the film sees Lucas engage in random acts of violence that serve little purpose to the overall story, focusing more on Lucas's chaotic and disorganized modus operandi. There's even a very open-ended conclusion, finishing before Lucas is even arrested, thus omitting the real-life event which saw Henry Lee Lucas confess to over 100 murders.

How did the film *Zodiac* differ from the real events?

Zodiac (2007) was one of the most critically acclaimed serial killer movies of all time, weaving an intricate plot that spanned an entire decade during the 1960s hunt for the infamous Zodiac killer.

The film touches upon all of the main components of the case, including Zodiac's multiple kills, his creepy phone call into a TV show, his cryptic ciphers, and Robert Graysmith, the cartoonist who became obsessed with solving the case. The film introduces multiple suspects, as happened in reality, but the real Zodiac killer's identity remains a mystery to this day.

One such suspect was a man named Arthur Leigh Allen; a former high school teacher disgraced for molesting children. Allen was a primary suspect in the Zodiac case, with much circumstantial evidence pointing toward him being the culprit. However, handwriting analysis of the Zodiac's letters eventually ruled Allen out.

The film version, however, makes it clear that Allen was indeed responsible for the Zodiac murders. The real Arthur Leigh Allen passed away in 1992, taking any guilt he might have harbored to his grave.

What unexplained phenomenon inspired the original *Nightmare on Elm Street?*

A Nightmare On Elm Street (1984) introduced the world to iconic villain Freddie Kruger, an otherworldly demon who murders people in their dreams. It sounds like a completely fabricated plotline, but the director of the film, Wes Craven, ripped the idea straight from the headlines.

Craven read a newspaper article about a child from the Cambodian genocide who kept himself awake for days on end, terrified that if he slept, he would be attacked in his dreams and never wake up again. The boy eventually fell asleep from exhaustion, and at last, his parents breathed a sigh of relief. But in the middle of the night, they heard their son screaming. When they reached him, he'd died.

Incredibly, this unexplained death wasn't a one-off. During the same period, around 20 Southeast Asian men mysteriously died in their sleep, and autopsies later found nothing medically wrong with these "victims." These bizarre deaths typically occurred in teenage to 30-year-old men, and more strangely, only seemed to occur in refugees on the island country of Laos.

The strange incident has not been explained, nor have any theories been put forward as to how the original victim somehow knew that going to sleep would result in his death.

Who killed his father and brother because he was inspired by a video game?

In 2016, 16-year-old Eldon Samuel killed his brother and father after being inspired by a character in the video game *Grand Theft Auto 5*. Samuel took a machete and stabbed his brother to death, then picked up two of his father's guns - a pistol and a shotgun - and shot him to death.

Strangely, it was Samuel's father who originally taught him how to be proficient with weapons. The family was "doomsday preppers," a colloquial term for those who prepare for the end-of-the-world scenarios.

Tina Samuel, Eldon's mother, explained how their family would practice "killing zombies." Samuel would regularly skip school, instead spending time at home watching horror movies and playing video games with the father he eventually killed.

But Eldon's main source of inspiration came from the video game *Grand Theft Auto 5*, in particular the character of Trevor Phillips - a violent drunk with a high gun proficiency. Eldon claimed that he wanted to be "just like Trevor." According to Eldon, the family were planning on packing everything up and moving into the mountains to "escape the zombies." Eldon was sentenced to life in prison despite being only 16 years old at the time of the murder.

CONCLUSION

As you've seen in this volume, serial killers are complex creatures that cover a broad range of personalities, characteristics, races, genders, and sexual orientations. Sex-starved deviants, rage-fueled sociopaths, deluded psychotics who live in their own torturous fantasy worlds - serial killers cover the length and breadth of the human spectrum.

Psychopaths are not all murderous brutes. Some serial killers commit atrocious acts for incredibly mundane reasons. Cannibals eat humans to appease feelings of loneliness. There are many more unsolved murders than there are solved ones. There are serial killers currently walking the streets right now. And of course, be wary of the next truck driver you come across.

Some of the information above might be common knowledge to the true crime aficionado, but we've dug deep into all available research materials, unearthing many obscure facts that we're sure will be news to even the most fanatical true crime fan. In fact, some of the information here has been reprinted for the first time in decades, with some tidbits hidden away in long-lost newspaper articles or media. And of course, we encourage you to dig deeper into any areas of trivia that appeal to you. There's a lot more obscure serial trivia out there to be unearthed.

The intention of this book is not to glamorize or glorify serial killers, nor to sensationalize their crimes or exploit their victims' tragedies. The fact remains that serial killers fascinate us all for myriad reasons, and many people seek to understand them for their own personal motives. Twisted minds are unfathomable and unknowable to any rational thinker, and that's what draws us toward these human monsters. Serial killing sits at the extreme of the human experience, which naturally allures the curious.

All of the trivia above details another person's tragedy, and we implore you to treat these subject matters with the courtesy they deserve. These are not stories to be exploited, but stories to be mulled over and learned from. Without these innocent victims, books like this wouldn't be possible, so we encourage readers to take a moment to honor and respect those who lost their lives.

We hope you've found something interesting in this book, whether it's learning about the psychopathic mind, killer children, human flesh-eaters, killer-inspired by works of fiction, or anything else. Our thoughts and respect go out to all of the victims who suffered at the hands of the homicidal monsters mentioned in this book, and we hope that our readers can learn a thing or two to ensure they don't suffer the same fate.

MORE BOOKS BY JACK ROSEWOOD

There is little more terrifying than those who hunt, stalk and snatch their prey under the cloak of darkness. These hunters search not for animals, but for the touch, taste, and empowerment of human flesh. They are cannibals, vampires and monsters, and they walk among us.

These serial killers are not mythical beasts with horns and shaggy hair. They are people living among society, going about their day-to-day activities until nightfall. They are the Dennis Rader's, the fathers, husbands, church going members of the community.

This A-Z encyclopedia of 150 serial killers is the ideal reference book. Included are the most famous true crime serial killers, like Jeffrey Dahmer, John Wayne Gacy, and Richard Ramirez, and not to mention the women who kill, such as Aileen Wuornos and Martha Rendell.

There are also lesser-known serial killers, covering many countries around the world, so the range is broad.

Each of the serial killer files includes information on when and how they killed the victims, the background of each killer, or the suspects in some cases such as the Zodiac killer, their trials and punishments. For some there are chilling quotes by the killers themselves.

The Big Book of Serial Killers is an easy-to-follow collection of information on the world's most heinous murderers.

Our first volume caused such an impact that we've decided to bring you the long-awaited Volume 2 of the most comprehensive Serial Killer encyclopedia ever published!

Murderers or monsters, normal people turned bad, or people born with the desire to kill; it doesn't matter where they come from, serial killers strike dread into our hearts with a single mention of their names. Hunting in broad daylight or stalking from the shadows, we are their prey, and their hunt is never done until they are caught or killed.

With a worrying number of them living in our communities, working alongside us at our places of employment and sharing the same spaces where we spend time with our families, serial killers are typically just another neighbor that we barely think about. A worrying thought, to be honest.

In The Big Book of Serial Killers Volume 2 we go through the lives of 150 serial killers who allowed themselves to fall under the influence of their darkest desires and took the lives anywhere from one to one hundred victims; we speak of their motives and how their stories ended (*if* they ended…), and remind you of the fear and pain that they left behind.

But what can you expect from **The Big Book of Serial Killers Volume 2?**

You will find such things as:

- ⊕ An excellent A-Z list of all of these deadly killers, allowing you to reference the encyclopedia whenever you need to find out more about any single murderer.
- ⊕ All of the uncensored details of their crimes, with much effort taken into account to describe their horrific acts.
- ⊕ Important information on their date and place of birth, date of arrest and number of victims, among other facts.
- ⊕ A list of Trivia facts for each killer, allowing you to learn more about their personalities and any films or documentaries made about them.

So, with nothing more to add – it's only time now for you purchase this book and begin learning about 150 of the sickest, most dangerous serial killers in world history.

This is the next level in murder: are you ready to learn about the evilest men and women in history?

Made in the USA
Las Vegas, NV
07 December 2022

61190753R00105